LEADERSHIP OF SHAME

LEADERSHIP OF SHAME

PLEADING "IGNORANCE OF THE LAW," AFTER HARMING ANOTHER IN REPRISAL, IS NO EXCUSE

GURINDER RANA

Notion Press

Old No. 38, New No. 6
McNichols Road, Chetpet
Chennai - 600 031

First Published by Notion Press 2018
Copyright © Gurinder Rana 2018
All Rights Reserved.

ISBN 978-1-948424-15-8

This book has been published with all reasonable efforts taken to make the material error-free after the consent of the author. No part of this book shall be used, reproduced in any manner whatsoever without written permission from the author, except in the case of brief quotations embodied in critical articles and reviews.

The Author of this book is solely responsible and liable for its content including but not limited to the views, representations, descriptions, statements, information, opinions and references ["Content"]. The Content of this book shall not constitute or be construed or deemed to reflect the opinion or expression of the Publisher or Editor. Neither the Publisher nor Editor endorse or approve the Content of this book or guarantee the reliability, accuracy or completeness of the Content published herein and do not make any representations or warranties of any kind, express or implied, including but not limited to the implied warranties of merchantability, fitness for a particular purpose. The Publisher and Editor shall not be liable whatsoever for any errors, omissions, whether such errors or omissions result from negligence, accident, or any other cause or claims for loss or damages of any kind, including without limitation, indirect or consequential loss or damage arising out of use, inability to use, or about the reliability, accuracy or sufficiency of the information contained in this book.

table of contents

preface	*vii*
acknowledgements	*xiii*
Chapter I	
the board of inquiry (day 1)	1
Chapter II	
examinations and cross-examinations (day 2)	20
Chapter III	
analysis of the case	62
Chapter IV	
conclusion	76

preface

"Thou shall not lie, cheat or steal, nor allow others to do so." This is the United States Army Officer Code of Conduct and every officer and soldier entering the United States Army takes an Oath to abide by this Code, both on and off duty. In fact, it is said that an Army Officer in the United States of America is never off-duty. The Army, as an institution, is so organized, rigid with codes, rules and regulations that there is no margin for deviation. If this was truly the case then, what exactly transpired in the Captain Arvind Johar (name changed) situation that left all that heard about this case in shock; who was at the core of such conspiracy and; why did the institution of the Army fail Captain Arvind Johar? The answers to these questions are a Lesson Learned.

By the year 2001, Captain Arvind Johar had earned many distinguished awards in the United States Army for outstanding performance of duties and for going above the call of duty. He was hailed as the "go-to person in tough or virtually impossible situations." Arvind was a class-act for peers and subordinates to emulate. He was multitalented, effective and efficient in whatever assignment he was given. He was a "solid performer in a multilevel organization and institution." Arvind always sought additional responsibility and made every one of them a success story. Even in the first part of 2001, before the arrival of Major Michael

Preface

Jackson Colors (MJ) (name changed), Arvind was deemed an asset to the Command and the Army. Then; what precisely happened after the arrival of MJ that changed Arvind's performance from a go-getter to "the worst officer in history," on a dime, if such downturn in performance actually did indeed take place; why did the Commander fail to intervene and assess; why didn't the Army investigate? The answers to these questions indicate a collapse of the organized system of the United States Army; again, this is another Lesson Learned.

On the 8th of September 2001, Captain Arvind Johar was recommended by his Commander, endorsed by his Group Commander and hailed by the General Officer (a Major General) for not only doing a superb job in his assigned duties, but for also performing the duties and responsibilities of his superiors in their absence, in an outstanding manner.

Then; on the 9th of September 2001, Major MJ Colors told Captain Arvind Johar that, "You, Captain, don't belong in my Army and, unless you resign your commission as an officer in my Army, I assure you that you will face my wrath." MJ said these threatening words to Arvind behind closed doors, because in the absence of others his threats fall under "Plausible Deniability."

In September 2003, at the first Board of Inquiry (BOI), MJ was questioned about his threatening remarks to his subordinate Captain Johar on the 9th of September 2001, behind closed doors. After a brief thought, MJ responded, "I don't recall."

A true Leader will own up to his mistakes and duly make course corrections in his leadership style, but not MJ; the Major hid behind that cloak of "Plausible Deniability" by simply claiming he did not remember his own fault. Such deniability is very doubtful.

Following the threats to life and livelihood, Arvind received three more derogatory counseling statements from MJ and in all these statements MJ quoted articles of the Uniform Code of Military Justice (UCMJ) against Arvind.

At the BOI in September 2003, MJ was questioned about those derogatory statements to which he replied that, "I was coaching the Captain to become a better leader."

Leaders don't coach subordinates using threats of capital or punitive punishment, especially when the subordinates have previously been hailed as assets to self, organization and institution alike. Leaders don't instill fear in their subordinates to make them perform. This is elementary in leadership class and so, it is obvious that MJ fudged his reply to conceal his actual intent; perhaps for fear that the institution will punish him instead.

In October 2001, Major MJ Colors ordered Captain Arvind Johar to undergo a Mental Health Evaluation (MHE), at the behest of a non-military third party. Arvind strongly objected and exercised his legal rights, but the Commander pushed Arvind to play along with MJ. This MHE was conducted by a non-military physician with over 25 years of expertise in the medical profession. After the MHE, the Doctor wrote to MJ, with a copy to the non-military third party, and made it clear that there was nothing wrong with Arvind's mental condition or thought processes. He further suggested that who-so-ever conceived such absurd allegations against Arvind should seek psychiatric examination.

The intent for which MJ had ordered Arvind to a Mental Health Examination (MHE) had backfired on both him and the Command. The Commander should have taken

Preface

notice and assessed the situation properly, so as to prevent any further embarrassments, but he was spineless; the Commander remained mum.

At the BOI in September 2003, MJ was questioned about the response he received from the non-military Mental Health Specialist, to whom he had sent Captain Arvind Johar, who was a subordinate. Again, MJ pleaded ignorance by claiming that, "I don't recall."

At the end of October 2001, MJ ordered Arvind to take an Army Physical Fitness Test (APFT). Arvind had already taken the APFT for the Record on the 18th of August 2001 and his grader was none other than the Commander himself. Arvind had passed that APFT in August and wasn't due for another test till, at least, February 2002. In accordance with the Army Field Manual on APFT, every Army personnel must take the APFT for the Record once every six months. In light of this, Captain Arvind Johar objected to this unnecessary and untimely APFT; he saw this APFT as another attempt to victimize him only, based on the turn of events in his life following the arrival of MJ in the Command.

In addition, Captain Arvind Johar was suffering from an acute foot problem that would medically prevent him from running and the Command was aware of this injury. However, still Major Colors insisted that Arvind must undergo another APFT and the Commander did exactly what he did prior to the MHE earlier; he pushed Arvind to take the test again.

The APFT was never the intent of MJ; this APFT was a vehicle to entrap Arvind. At the ground, Arvind met two non-commissioned officers; both African-Americans. One non-commissioned officer (NCO) took Arvind aside and offered to pass the Captain, if this superior officer agreed to pay the NCO a hundred dollars. The NCO informed the Captain that he had four kids and a wife that he has to feed, and his military pay was insufficient.

The assessment Captain Arvind Johar arrived at was that the NCO had been pushed into doing this illegal act and perhaps he had been threatened with dire consequences, if he refused. The speech was a recital of words; it was not the normally used by that NCO.

To make a long story short, Arvind refused to pay for a pass on the APFT. He clearly rejected the offer to bribe or be involved in any other illegal activity. Arvind also warned the NCO to refrain himself from such future thoughts, or else he will be forced to report the NCO.

The APFT never took place; it was hatched to entrap Captain Arvind Johar in an illegal act, whereby those three counseling statements mentioning articles of the UCMJ would prove true and then, MJ would recommend Arvind to be relieved from the Army with a Dishonorable Discharge. This was the wrath MJ had perceived against Arvind; however, Arvind miraculously realized it and again, another attempt against him backfired.

In December 2001, Arvind was supposed to depart for school with onward movement for Blocked Leave to see his aging parent and to prepare for his sibling's marriage, which had been preapproved by the Commander. MJ withheld Arvind's travel orders, until after the course had begun and then, falsely claimed that, "The Captain chose leave over school." This course was a must for Arvind to execute his assigned duties in the deployment of teams in support of national contingency operations. Arvind was harmed, without just cause.

The Group Command and Arvind knew that Captain Arvind Johar had never made such claims as presented by

MJ, but the training was missed and the Captain was left handicapped.

The Major was quizzed on the stand at the BOI in September 2003 about his withholding of those training orders from the subordinate, a subordinate officer.

At first MJ claimed that Arvind failed the APFT and so, he did not allow a failure to embarrass the Command at school.

The Defense Team quickly countered this response by demanding MJ to produce the Official APFT Scorecard prescribed under the Army Field Manual and Army Regulation.

MJ then, tried to lay blame on the two non-commissioned officers, by claiming they had informed him that the Captain had failed the APFT.

The Defense Team quickly realized that MJ was saying he actually had no first-hand account of an APFT failure in this case; it was all hearsay. They addressed this to the Board.

Almost instantly, the Prosecution objected claiming that MJ was not the one on trial. After this, one of the board members rose to his feet and made the following very damning statement for the Prosecution: "If our brief is to find the Defendant guilty then, we are wasting our time here." The Prosecution urgently called a recess, following this remark.

What are your thoughts; should Arvind be found guilty or not; was the BOI the correct course of action, prior to concluding an investigation in this case? Thanks!

acknowledgements

I would personally be honored to appreciate the characters in this true account, whose name have been altered, changed or amended to protect them. I am sure after reading this account the characters will identify themselves and try to make a counterattack, which is reprisal against free speech. My intent is not to spark controversy; my intent is to coach.

Honoring my parents and my brother is hardly enough for their patience, their assistance in reviewing my works and their untiring commitment to my success. I can fall and fail many times and my family will always be there to lift me up and encourage me to achieve my goals. I love them from the bottom of my heart and in my soul. Thank you.

I would be amiss to forget my spouse, who helped me in constructing the framework of this case, gathering the evidence and coherently piecing the puzzle together. I am ever indebted to her.

Leadership is a skill that is earned and the covenants of leadership are to be followed. Leadership is of two types: (1) Good and enjoyable; (2) bad and shameful. My first book, "Rise to Fame" is of the first kind and this manuscript is of the second. I hope you like them.

Lastly; I cherish my relationship with Notion Press for turning my spark to become an Author into reality. Your connection reflects the great spirit of propelling amateurs to experts. Thank you Notion Press.

CHAPTER I

the board of inquiry
(day 1)

Date: 21st September 2003

Venue: Headquarters, 99th Regional Support Command, Coraopolis, Pennsylvania

Style of Board Announced: Verbatim Proceedings

Charges brought against Captain Arvind Johar (name changed):

1. Several Instances of AWOL (absence without leave), from his place of duty on Fort Meade, in October 2002;
2. Groggy Appearance;
3. Poor Performance;
4. Misconduct; altering own DD Form 689 (Quarter's Slip).

Prosecuting Attorney: Captain Jon Huddle (name changed)

Defense Attorneys: Phil (a respected civil lawyer) and Dave (a junior Army Reserve Judge Advocate; a Captain)

The Boardroom, which is usually the Command Conference Room, for these verbatim proceedings, had been haphazardly conceived in the Pantry on the ground floor. On one side was the Defense Team and on the other was the Prosecution. Directly across from the entry was a stage with a two party tables covered with a cloth and four chairs behind it for the Panel of Judges. Entering the room; directly across from the stage was a professional recording apparatus complete with amplifier and controls. Next to this was a chair for the Legal Advisor to the Board. The room was cramped for space; it was definitely not the ideal venue.

The Prosecutor and Defense took their seats, only to rise again as the Panel of Judges entered the room, along with their Legal Advisor, and took their places on the stage. The Defense and Prosecution took their seats thereafter. The Hearing was underway and; Arvind began to feel the chill of concern.

The Board President (a female Army Colonel) turned to the Legal Advisor (another Army Colonel; a Judge Advocate) and asked, "How is it done, Mike?"

The Legal Advisor rose to his feet and calmly explained that the Board must address the decorum to be followed in these proceedings, so that there is no ambiguity and the process remains smooth. He then, enlightened the Panel on stage (a Colonel and three Lieutenant Colonels) about the Prosecutorial Brief in the Opening that is to be followed by the Defense. He, finally, turned to the Prosecution and Defense asking them to add any substance he might have missed.

Captain Huddle (the Prosecutor) had nothing to add and so, he released his time to the Defense to add substance, if they saw it fit to do so.

Dave (the Defense Attorney and junior Judge Advocate) rose to his feet and reminded the Board that these proceedings were announced as 'Verbatim' and so; the Prosecution must assure this Board that the chosen recording devices are fully operational, because in such 'Verbatim Hearing' it is elementary that, following these proceedings, the Defense is provided with a copy of the 'Verbatim Audiotapes,' so that 'Due Process of the Law' is afforded to the Defendant in this case.

Phil (the Lead Attorney for the Defense) rose and directed the Prosecution to playback the recordings till now, just for assurance.

The Prosecutor objected on the grounds of 'Trust.'

Suddenly; there was pin-drop silence in the room, as the four attorneys sat staring at each other in all shock and awe. It was as though they were unable to believe their own ears.

Then; one of the more active Board members (a Lieutenant Colonel) broke the silence, asking the Legal Advisor "Is there such an obnoxious objection in jurisprudence as 'Trust'?"

The Legal Advisor responded in the negative; *"I haven't heard of 'Trust' as a legal grounds for an objection."*

The visibly displeasured Board Member overruled the objection citing "ex turpi causa non oritur actio" (latin for an action will not arise from disgraceful basis and distrust means suspicion; there is no suspicious element in asking for assurance in verbatim proceedings). This Lieutenant Colonel (LTC) went on to say "We are all trustworthy, until we are proven untrustworthy by the preponderance of the evidence before an appropriate Court of Justice."

The Legal Advisor quickly jumped to his feet and agreed with the Board, but then, claimed that it was only fair to afford the Prosecution a "Second Chance" to restate his objection. He directed Captain (CPT) Huddle to rephrase his objection to assurance requested for by the Defense.

CPT Huddle, in rephrasing his objection, claimed that the Prosecutor has the duty of ensuring audible tapes of the proceedings, with a degree of latitude and trust.

As both Defense attorneys rose to their feet, the now irate Board Member demanded to know that, if the Prosecutor is doing all he should to ensure due process to the Defendant in this case then, *"why is the Prosecutor denying the Defense assurance?"* He exclaimed, in frustration, "that it made absolutely no sense."

The Legal Advisor then, directed the Prosecution to reply the audiotape for the Defense.

The result was that the audiotape recorded something that was so faint that it was practically inaudible. The Prosecutor had a 'deer in the headlight' look about him; his objection proved that he had something to hide. These were just the beginnings of the 'Verbatim Hearing' in this case and none of the witnesses had taken the stand yet.

The Defense attorneys approached the Bench and demanded relief for CPT Arvind Johar on the grounds that the Prosecution had corrupted this case from the outset.

In his own defense, the CPT Huddle argued that he was unaware that the audio recording system was inoperative; he claimed he had tested the recording device a day earlier. CPT Huddle moved the Board to continue proceedings and allow for a 'Summary Judgment' in the case. The Defense strongly objected, citing that such change only served to deny their client of his 'Legal Due Process Rights.'

The Board President (a female Army Colonel), realizing that the matter was hot and rapidly reaching a brawl, quickly announced a recess for 15 minutes. She asked the Prosecution to remain behind with the Legal Advisor. The Defense (Dave) moved the Board to afford the Defendant representation of the proceedings, but the President denied that request on the grounds that the sidebar was only for internal Command and Staff.

All this while, Arvind had been sitting in his seat watching, absorbing and realizing the hard fact that he was now the target of this Command. This Command would go to any extent to prove that he was a 'bad apple' and a disgrace to the Armed Forces. Till the 8th of September 2001, CPT Arvind Johar was the 'cream of the crop' and today, this Command wanted to shunt him out as though he were 'an infectious cancer.' Although he had done so much good in the Army, Arvind felt like a failure on that unfortunate day in September 2003. His intellect kept asking him, "What have you truly earned after serving all these years; what is your life worth today?" Poor Arvind had no answer for himself; he was totally confused and it was a terrible feeling, to say the very least. He finally reasserted himself and told his wits that "those wacky officers are all hypocrites, but the whole Army isn't this bad."

Phil, Dave and Arvind quietly rose and exited the room, while the Captain Huddle, the Legal Advisor and the Board members remained behind for a heart-to-heart on strategy.

Suddenly Dave got a tickle in his head. He informed Phil that, as a matter of fact, that Dave, as a Staff Judge Advocate ("SJA") belonged to the Command and Staff, which affords him to be present in the Boardroom for the ongoing discussions. Dave was concerned that somehow the Prosecution might try to influence the Board members and the Legal Advisor would allow it, which would be detrimental to the Defense strategy. "We need to know what is discussed behind those doors and walls," Dave stated to Phil.

Phil didn't take even a second to agree and dispatched Dave to do the needful. Phil gave Dave specific instructions too.

Behind the mess hall the Command had setup a coffee table for the Board, to which Phil and Arvind quickly and quietly made their way.

After each got his coffee, both Phil and Arvind moved swiftly into a corner, away from earshot. Then; Phil explained to Arvind that the Prosecution didn't actually have any case and so, in his opinion, the Prosecution had invented hurdles to stall the inevitable outcome in the case. Phil called it "Huddle's Hurdles."

For a moment Arvind chewed on the words chanted by Phil; Arvind tried to laugh at the joke. However, Arvind had lost his willingness to laugh at jest; these were troubled waters for him and he knew it. In his mind, Arvind kept pondering the question "Is this, what I deserve, after all these years serving this nation, serving the people and, following the rules?" On the one hand; he knew that he had been the victim of prejudice in the workplace and on the other; he was convinced that his Defense Team would save him from that evil. Even if his Defense failed to deliver, the Team would have put in its best efforts to succeed.

Dave joined Phil and Arvind some ten minutes later and explained that Prosecution was going to introduce the Inspector General ("IG") complaint submitted by Arvind to attempt to sway the Board into believing that Arvind had falsely accused Major Colors of "Adultery." And; if that fails to convince the Board then, Prosecution will introduce the preliminary inquiry prepared by the Command IG in this case.

Phil took a minute to respond. He said, "All this would be Subjudice, since the Army IG is still investigating this case." In addition, he said, "The Command attempted twice to gain the permission of the Army IG for use of those investigative reports and, the Army IG denied the Command IG use of those documents. What is the confusion then?"

Dave replied, "I fully agree Phil, but we were not allowed to interject, object or participate in those discussions inside; we were observers only."

One of the Command members approached the trio, which halted all case-related discussions. There was exchange of pleasantries and then, it was time to return to the grind in the Boardroom.

The President of the Board began by addressing both sides, she said, "We are very sorry for the disruption, yet it was necessary. I wanted you all to know this fact. After discussion, some advice and counseling, the Prosecutor will rephrase his Opening Statement. Since the recording device is not operational at this time, we shall move on and at the end we can discuss our options."

Phil was not at all excited about the Board's decision; he rose to his feet and objected. He said, "This Board, as I recall, is supposed to be a verbatim hearing. Hence, it is not only required, but it is elementary that the Prosecution make reliable and reasonable arrangements to ensure verbatim proceedings in this case. Without these verbatim tapes, my Client is being denied his due process rights and that is unacceptable Colonel."

The Legal Advisor (another Colonel) rose to his feet in defense of his peer. He argued, "In jurisprudence, the Board has the last say on the conduct of the proceedings and the President of this Board has spoken. Let us proceed, please."

Phil turned to the Legal Advisor and reminded the Colonel that "In jurisprudence the Court or the Board, in this case, cannot redefine the type of hearing which will take place; these are announced prior to commencement of the Board or Court."

Captain Huddle, seeing an opportunity, jumped to his feet and said to Phil, "When a mistake is made by

Leadership of Shame

subordinates, leaders commonly afford those subordinates a second chance."

Huddle had just opened a fresh can of worms for himself; because both Phil and Dave were going to pounce on Jon Huddle with such might that even dynamite would not save him.

Dave, for a split second, was shocked to hear the Prosecutor making such statement that was obviously contradictory to his own strategy. He thought to himself, "Is the Command conceding its case? Then; Dave asked Huddle, "I am not sure whether you realize your own statement Jon, but if I am to understand your statement correctly, you are saying that you deserve another chance because you are a subordinate. If this is the case then, Arvind deserves a second chance too, don't you think? The rules are equal for all, I believe."

Captain Huddle seemed very perplexed at Dave's insinuation; he was rattled, in-fact. Jon Huddle replied to Dave in a strong tone, "Your client got many chances and I am only moving this Board for one; there is no comparison."

Now, Phil jumped into the ring in support of Dave. He reminded the Prosecution, "Jon Huddle, you claim that Captain Johar got many chances. Can you please elaborate for the Board? Let us begin with the charge of AWOL (absent without leave). How many times was Arvind AWOL Jon? Kindly enlighten us."

Captain Jon Huddle was visibly shaken by Phil's and Dave's attacks. He had definitely opened a can of worms for himself this time. Replying to Phil, "Your client was AWOL twice, according to the record."

Phil jeered at Huddle and said, "Jon, I am giving to a second chance to answer my question; "By the preponderance of the evidence, how many time has Arvind been AWOL?"

The Prosecution was lost for words; he was dumbfounded.

The President, from her pulpit on stage, attempted to break-up the verbal sidebar going on within the Board. However, the Prosecutor had put his own foot in his own mouth and Defense was taking advantage of the opportunity. Nothing wrong with that, is there?

The Legal Advisor, finally, broke-up the sidebar redirecting both sides to address the Board. He reminded both sides that the possibility of "Contempt" is a charge that the Board has a legal right to hold against either party to this case. The intended audience was not the Prosecution, but the Defense.

Once again the Boardroom was calm and composed. The President looked at the clock and pronounced that starting with Prosecution, both sides will present their Opening Statements, after which it will be time to adjourn proceedings for the day.

Arvind sat and pondered over what had been achieved during this Board process in one full eight-hour day. He began jotting down his thoughts on a piece of paper, still alert to the mumbo-jumbo of the hearing in the background. He had lost interest in the hair-splitting, really. Arvind is simple; he despises confusion in his life and, this cavil was not his brand of business at all.

The Prosecutor rose again. This time he held a writing pad in his hand. The Prosecutor stand at the podium and the following was his Opening Statement:

> *"Madam President and honorable Board members; you have all read the brief and you*

> *have all been briefed by the Commander. There should be no confusion. This Board has been convened against the Accused Defendant and this Board must find him guilty on all charges, because this is what your Commander wants. That is all."*

On the face of it, nothing appears wrong with the Prosecution's opening statement; however, in legal parlance, that opening statement appeared to be in violation of the tenants of jurisprudence. Prosecution seemed to have skipped Elementary Law classes from the looks of things. Defense was, once again, taking advantage of another mistake made by Captain Jon Huddle, the Prosecutor in this case.

Phil leapt to his feet in a jiffy. He said to Jon, "You mean the Major General has directed this Board to find my client guilty on all charges without trial? Please confirm."

Huddle was knocked for six yet again. He replied, *"That is not what I said. The Defense is purposely misrepresenting my statements."*

Phil sighed and turned to the Bench on stage; *"This is why it is mandatory to have verbatim tapes of these proceedings. The Prosecution can keep changing his statements without verbatim replay of his mention. Therefore; Defense moves this Board to recess, until Prosecution can assure us of the presence of proper operational recording and playback devices. This is a point to be noted."*

The President of the Board assured the parties that **"Defense's objection to the absence of proper recording and playback devices has been noted and will be taken into account. The Prosecution will ensure that the Boardroom is properly equipped for tomorrow. We don't wish to waste** *precious time arguing about 'verbatim' again. Defense; kindly present your opening remarks."*

Phil jumped to his feet and the following were his Opening Remarks:

"Lady and Gentlemen of this Board; let me begin by stating that this is a sham in jurisprudence. The Prosecution has made it sufficiently clear that this Board is plagued with unlawful disturbances. These illicit turbulences are due to 'Undue Command Influence,' which is in violation of Articles of the Uniform Code of Military Justice (UCMJ). The Prosecution is so rash that it has forgotten to clearly state the grounds; the charges for which we are here today. Therefore, the Defense will cure this impetuous mistake for the Prosecution.

The Defendant stands before this Board of Inquiry (BOI) on four allegations alone. These four allegations are these: (1) AWOL; (2) Groggy Appearance; (3) Misconduct for altering his own quarter's slip and; (4) Poor Performance. The dates are critical and vital in this case, because each and every accusation has been reported in October 2002, just prior to the conduct of an EMHE against the Defendant in this case. Discussion or decision on the EMHE is Subjudice, because this is under investigation by the SAIG and the DODIG at this time. The SAIG has denied this Command use of any of its investigative matter in this Board and, this is a major point to be noted.

During the course of this Hearing, Prosecution must prove by the preponderance of the evidence each and every charge this Command has made against the Defendant in this case. Absent evidence, it will be a grave injustice upon the Defendant to pronounce him 'Guilty,' regardless of what precisely the Commander of this outfit wants.

The Defense will evidence the fact that the Defendant in this case was never AWOL; that the Defendant was always professional in his ways; that the Defendant in this case never altered his own quarter's slip and; that the Defendant's performance, if poor, was purely due to his poor Leadership that mismanaged him and victimized him.

I will now turn the floor over to my learned and able colleague, Dave, for any addition."

Phil returned to his seat and Dave took to the floor. As Dave was posed to address the Board, the Prosecutor jumped to his feet and said, **"Government Objects."**

Phil rose again from his seat and moved to the center of the floor. He asked the Captain Jon Huddle, "*On what grounds is the Government objecting to now?*"

Jon Huddle seemed dazed by Phil's question. He took a few seconds to recompose himself. Then, he turned to face the Board. Captain Huddle explained, *"I have only stated the facts. This case is not about the faults of Government; this case is about Captain Arvind Johar and his lack of professionalism, which is why he is before this Board today."*

Both Phil and Dave gleamed at each other and then, turned to the Legal Advisor. Dave asked the Legal Advisor, *"Sir; would you like the honor of explaining to Prosecution that the Defendant is not guilty, until Government can convincingly prove, beyond a shadow of doubt, by the preponderance of the evidence, that the Defendant deserves punishment. Will you enlighten Captain Huddle or should the Defense do this too?"*

The whole jargon of jurisprudence seemed like a vast amount of haggling; a barter to win each and every point. This process was extremely time-consuming and nerve-wrecking for Arvind, who had been quietly perched in his chair throughout the entire ordeal watching and listening to this incoherent mumbo-jumbo. This was the lowest point in his entire 40 years; he had never been the subject or witness of such inefficiency.

The Prosecutor, once again, opened his impulsive mouth. He said, *"This Board was convened at the behest of the Commander (a Major General); she told the Board members that they need to find the Defendant in this case guilty, because she does not wish to accommodate a non-deployable asset in her Command. I have not said anything wrong."*

Finally; the Board member on the extreme right of the Bench rose to his feet and said, **"If the Commander has already made up her mind to convict this Defendant then, it is a waste of our valuable time to be here. Prosecution should simply go ahead and pronounce the Defendant 'Guilty as Charged,' without a Hearing. I will not become part to such unethical proceedings; I lack the time for it."**

With that; the irate Board member left the Bench and headed for the door. On the way to the exit, he paused briefly by Arvind to say **"Best of Luck Captain."**

Arvind turned and rose to his feet saying, "Much-appreciated Sir."

The Board President and the rest of her Bench rose and declared the Hearing closed for the day. She announced that this Board would reconvene the next morning at eight. The Colonel reminded the Prosecution to ensure his part and advised him to leave behind any comic appendage the Prosecution has left up his sleeve. She added that in the morning the Board would reconvene to hear the witnesses, their examinations and the cross-examinations. The Colonel made it crystal-clear to all that **"Tomorrow, we have a full day guys."**

Adjourned; the Defense, along with its witnesses exited the halls of this Command Headquarters for the day. There was much to be discussed and preparations of the witnesses were rife in the air. Quietly and swiftly; the Defense Team moved by road to their hotel, the Embassy Suites atop the hill. All left the vehicles and headed to their individual rooms to freshen up and rest awhile. Phil informed all, prior to their departure that both he and Dave would work with the witnesses independently. Dave told Arvind to relax and wait in his room for his call; he said, *"We will get together with Phil later this evening, perhaps for dinner."* With these marching orders, the Team dispersed from the parking lot.

Phil and Dave met with each of the four Defense witnesses and prepared them for every possible eventuality that could possibly transpire at the Board on 'Day Two.' Dave was pretty confident that the preparations were perfectly done, the best any attorney could do. Phil was a bit more moderate and chose to wait and see what happens; Phil is an experienced military attorney with two decades or more in practice. He was also a Navy Commander in the U.S. Naval Reserves at the time.

Arvind went back to his room; freshened up a bit and changed into his physical training gear. He was going to the gym for a short workout before dinner. Arvind had planned to gym, shower and change, and then join Phil and Dave later.

In the gym, Arvind walked in on two of his seniors, who were both Government witnesses. For a brief moment, Arvind thought of skipping his gym workout. However; since he had done nothing wrong, he had nothing to be afraid of in this case. He got on to the jogger and began his workout. The two seniors were none other than Lieutenant Colonel ("LTC") Caesar Augustus (name changed), who was Arvind's Commander and Major M.J. Colors. Major Colors made the following statement to LTC Augustus:

"Some subordinates are real jerks and should be hung to death by their nuts."

There was no response from the LTC, but the LTC smiled backed at the Major. Perhaps this is the way superior officers in the military give their approval on inappropriate behavior, thought Arvind.

Captain Johar continued to work out. He moved from the jogger to the dumbbells and then, finished off with some stretching.

Throughout his workout, the two seniors kept making remarks that were border line unprofessional. This was the Major's approach to try and instigate Arvind into argument and, Arvind knew this all too well. The Captain resisted biting the bullet this time and avoided any intended altercation with his superiors. He knew that the Major was on a malicious streak, because the day, in the morning, he would take the stand.

Phil, Dave and Arvind met in the bar for a drink before dinner. The Defense witnesses were nowhere in sight. This was most likely the tactic engaged by the Defense attorneys to avoid any untoward activities, since the Prosecutorial witnesses were staying in the same hotel. Arvind thought the approach was perfect.

Over dinner, the three discussed strategy for the next day. Phil was sure that Huddle would put Colors on the stand first. In his view, Colors would suggest that Arvind was AWOL and that he had altered his own quarter's slip.

Dave added that the Defense would cross-examine Colors with the evidence from the Head Nurse and other medical experts.

Phil urgently pointed out that the list of witnesses provided by Prosecution did not include any medical personnel and Defense has none too. He was pointing to an obvious problem.

Dave asked Phil whether it was legally possible to stall proceedings in order to summon the medical witnesses.

Phil replied in the negative, saying most likely Huddle would object and the Legal Advisor would support him.

Phil and Dave re-read the statements from the doctors and the Head Nurse on the AWOL and altered quarter's slip. Dave then, handed the statements over to Arvind for his perusal.

Dave was clear that the statements were straightforward and mincing words, although possible, would be pretty difficult to do, especially for Huddle.

Phil agreed with Dave and moved on to the next issue. He said the issue on 'Groggy Appearance' is extremely vague, not to mention unsupported.

Dave argued that 'Groggy Appearance,' in the military, refers to unprofessional appearance and so, it could only be wear and appearance of uniform, shaving, shoe shining and other minor problems for which many junior enlisted soldiers tend to be punished. This is not common in the commissioned officer ranks, he added.

Phil was on a different track all together. He suggested that the Command meant that Arvind presented an unstable look; like one would find in a drunk or drugged soldier.

This approach jolted a thought in Dave's brain. He reminded Phil that Colors had reported that Arvind was illegally taking prescribed drugs, which were prescribed medication, in-fact.

Arvind added that Major Colors had ordered him to a MHE in October 2001 based on an identical report and Colors had recommended Arvind for another MHE in May 2002, according to the evidence provided by the Prosecution in this case. Arvind added that Major Colors was behind the suspension of his security clearance and the essay documented on the Army Form was generally the same as the essay presented by Colors in May 2002 and in October 2001.

Phil absorbed all this information, carefully sifted through it, documented points and then, addressed both Dave and Arvind. He said, according to the information you both have provided, Colors is central to this MHE/EMHE saga; Colors is the mastermind behind them. If I am reading it properly, the EMHE conducted against Arvind in October 2002 was premeditated.

Dave replied in the affirmative. However, he also stated that the three of them had deviated from the main discussion, 'Groggy Appearance.' Dave asked Arvind for his thoughts.

Arvind reminded both Phil and Dave that Groggy meant tired, fatigued and dazed in the dictionary. Appearance is looks. He added that an officer that was victimized, hassled, mismanaged and thrown away like garbage would feel, look and act fatigued and tired; such an officer will not wish to work under that leadership for sure.

Both Phil and Dave agreed with Arvind one hundred percent. Phil made it crystal-clear that this would be their stand in the morning. Dave seconded Phil's decision and Arvind became a Saint (in jest).

As Phil, Dave and Arvind were concluding dinner, Augustus and Colors eased their way on to the adjoining table. Phil signaled his two counterparts and the discussions went on sudden hold. Dinner over; the three walked around for a bit and retreated to Phil's room for the conclusion of discussions. The remainder of the discussions was 'Poor Performance.'

Leadership of Shame

Back in Phil's cabin, seated around the table, the trio engaged in some fierce debate on 'Poor Performance.' They hashed out every ounce of dirt on the issue and thrashed out every grain of filth contained in Arvind's evaluation reports. At last, Dave concluded that post Arvind's detail to a sister concern his performance was reported as outstanding; superb and; helpful. This he said proves that in a different command serving under a separate commander, Arvind would shine. Dave explained that this was in the regulation, which the Command failed to follow.

Aha, exclaimed Phil; we are on the right track now. This is not about 'Poor Performance' at all; this is about 'Poor Leaders and Poor Leadership.' This made Dave king (figuratively speaking).

Having thrashed-out the main charges in this case, Phil made it crystal-clear to his two understudies that in the event Huddle attempted to introduce IG matter in the Board, Defense would strongly object and exit the Hearing. Dave agreed, without protest. This was all in Arvind's favor, so he had no objections either. The trio adjourned their discussions for the night and retreated to their individual rooms for some rest, ahead of a more grueling day; the examinations and cross-examinations of witnesses.

I want to add here that; years later, a decade after this Board, Arvind contemplated the reason why leaders don't put their understudies first or only focus on just a select few. He concluded that nations are reactive and not proactive; leaders focus on a select few that are close to them and treat the rest as step-children (in an alternative manner of speaking). If leaders focused on the People, their safety, their security and their development then, terror or corruption would have no grounds to exist. This is not about Republicans or Democrats in the United States and this is not about the Gandhi Dynasty or the Bharatiya Janta Party ("BJP"), this is all about the People, the Society, the Communities and the Nation.

People are of different races, religions, creeds and genders; this does not mean that the Caucasian race is separate from the African-Americans or the Indians. A Muslim is no different than a Christian, in reality; leaders need to sit through a class on World Religions. A woman is no weaker than men in today's business world; in fact, many women lead multinational organizations and are extremely successful. Transgender and Gays are a way of life, which culture should embrace. Leaderships that are successful are those that embrace the proposal that best ideas evolve from the lowest ranks of employment. Even an office boy can provide a great idea to efficiently manage interoffice exchanges, the pantry and the housekeeping. This can save organizations a ton of dough. Therefore; leave no one behind, because everyone has a capability and a responsibility to others, he thought.

Perhaps, if leaders pick the brains of this guide, problems like North Korea, Pakistan and Iran can be solved. This dynamite of a walking dictionary of ideas may have solutions to assist in refreshing rivers in India and making it tough to acquire a gun or explosives in the United States. Arvind is a Leader in my books, but will he become one in your eyes? Let us wait and see.

CHAPTER II

examinations and cross-examinations /day 2/

Sharp at eight; Defense was standing fast outside the makeshift Boardroom in an Army Command Headquarters in Coraopolis, PA. The Defense witnesses, five now, had congregated on the couches inside the entrance to the building. Prosecution was nowhere in sight yet, but one Government witness was seen making his way towards the Prosecutor's office. There was pin-drop silence in the hallway outside the Boardroom; "...*we could hear each other breathing,*" Arvind said. There was a sense of victory and a sense of defeat in the Defense camp that morning.

At half past eight, Captain Jon Huddle walked up the hallway and greeted the Defense; he acknowledged Arvind too and reminded his peer that he was just doing his job and that he had no adverse feelings toward him. Although just words, these words perked up the Defense Team and once again the gloves were back on the hands. Both sides were ready to spar with each other once more. Huddle announced that Board would begin in 30 minutes. He also informed Defense counsels that coffee and tea were available in the back as on the previous day. Jon welcomed the Defense to enjoy the moment.

At nine; Jon Huddle entered the makeshift Boardroom and ordered "All Rise." Defense and Defendant rose and welcomed the Board members; exchanged pleasantries with the Prosecution and; greeted the Legal Advisor, as is customary in every military outfit. Defense and Prosecution waited patiently for the Board to take their places on the stage. Once seated, Defense warmed their chairs again; however, Prosecution remained standing.

The President of the Board directed her first missile of a question at the Prosecutor. She said to him, **"Captain Huddle; have you ensured this Board has an operational recording and playback device; can this Board have a demo please, if you will?"**

The Prosecutor appeared to have gone into shock; he seemed traumatized by the Colonel's request for a demo. Jon Huddle had a deer in the headlight look; he was staring at the Defense, as if his opposition was about to give him the key to his success.

Just then; Phil rose and asked Prosecution, *"Have you heard the Colonel, Jon; kindly proceed with the demo."*

This dramatized scene continued for all of ten minutes, when suddenly the Prosecutor regained consciousness, apparently. He did not acknowledge the question of the Board President nor did he react to Defense. All in the room wondered whether the Prosecutor had suffered temporary unconsciousness or whether his lack of awareness was dramatized. Defense saw this act as a convenient ploy to earn sympathy of the Board.

The Prosecutor said, *"Government calls its first witness, Major M.J. Colors. This witness is a key witness and will..."*

Without allowing Jon Huddle to finish his speech, the Board President interrupted saying, *"Stop Captain! This quorum is incomplete and so, we cannot proceed without a replacement for LTC Marco De Souza. In addition to that, we need a demo on the recording apparatus you have acquired for this session of the Proceedings. Thanks."*

Time was closing in on 1030 hours; examinations and cross-examinations of the witnesses were still in the balance. The technical difficulties experienced in this Board were unparallel to any other legal proceedings the Defense attorneys had ever witnessed; to them, this was a sure shot sham.

The Prosecution approached the Bench and requested 10 minutes to complete the Quorum and to produce a verbatim recording device. Dave strongly objected on the grounds that this Board had already been in session for a day and the Prosecution is still not ready. The Legal Advisor came to the assistance of the Prosecution, but Phil interrupted to give Dave a boost. This debate before the Bench stretched for 15 minutes and at 1045 hours the Board President announced a 15-minute recess to allow Prosecution to make amends.

Over coffee; Phil made it very unambiguous that Prosecution was employing dramatics to forestall the Proceedings, in an attempt to force the Board to pronounce a guilty verdict. Dave saw things slightly differently. He thought that Prosecution was unprepared, because Jon Huddle had no intention of allowing a verbatim Hearing in this case. Generally; Defense noticed the pretense of Prosecution and decided that disallow it any further.

Back in the Boardroom; a fresh face appeared on the Bench, another female officer. Phil rose and objected stating that Prosecution had not provided the replacement officer's name to the Defense and the Defense was denied the chance to depose of this replacement.

The Prosecution countered Defense stating that this replacement was on the list of alternatives he was given the night before. He requested the Board for leniency. The Prosecution went on to explain that he was only informed the night before this Board that he would be prosecuting.

Dave was not impressed at all. He strongly objected stating this was not Defense's problem; it was a Command issue, which must not be used to harm the Defendant in this case.

The Legal Advisor was of the opinion that enough time had been afforded to Prosecution to make amends, but then left the final decision on the Board.

At last, at 1100 hours, precisely; the Board President, finally, ended the travesty before the Bench. *"The Command announced and convened this Board and so, therefore, the onus to ensure the Board was technically free of issues lies with the Command,"* she said. *"However, this Board is of the view that this Hearing must continue,"* she added. *"Hopefully, Prosecution has employed an operational recording device for the remainder of these Proceedings,"* she concluded.

Obviously; the decision of the Board was in favor of Prosecution and against the Defense. Phil wanted this to be noted on tape and replayed, but the Board President wanted to allow a level of trust that Prosecution had made amends over the break. Perhaps she was impressed with Prosecution for completing the Quorum in record time. Who knows?

Prosecution began, *"My first witness is Government's key witness in this case and I had like to add that he must catch a flight in an hour back to West Point in Upstate New York."*

Both Phil and Dave jumped to their feet, *"Objection; the Government convened this Board against our client and this Board was announced in March of this year, which is almost 180 days ago. Government should have arranged schedules to coincide with requirements of this legal process. Defense has every right to cross-examine this witness,"* said Phil.

Dave added, *"Our client, the Defendant in this case, has not vacated his Rights to Due Process. Defense has a Right to depose and cross Government witnesses and time must not become a restriction in the process."*

The Legal Advisor intervened on behalf of the Board and said, **"The Rights of Defense will not be a restriction at all; however, this Board must be concluded by COB today at the very latest. Therefore, we should get on with it."**

Arvind sitting back in his chair observed that each time there was a scuffle between Prosecution and Defense before the Bench, the decisions made by the Board President or the Legal Advisor seemed to be in favor of Prosecution. This Board appeared to have been rigged from the outset.

Major Colors took the stand.

Prosecution approached him and asked, *"Good morning Major Colors, Sir; trust you had a pleasant stay at the Embassy Suites last night. So; kindly enlighten this Board about Captain Arvind Johar,"* he said.

Major Colors replied, *"The Defendant is the worst officer and soldier I have ever served with in the United States Army and I have been in the Army for 11 years now."*

Prosecution then asked, *"Why do you feel that the Defendant in this case is the worst officer, Major?"*

The Major responded, *"Captain Johar was AWOL on several occasions, as I have reported previously; he altered his own Quarter's slip, which is misconduct and unbecoming of* a commissioned officer, and; he is always fighting against his chain of command, which is stressful. To give an example, the Defendant submitted a 130+ page IG complaint against his Command. He didn't have to do that, he could have consulted with his leadership first."

Prosecution further probed, "You reported that the Defendant in this case was AWOL on the 6th of October 2002, is this correct and is this signature on this form your's Sir?"

Major Colors replied, "It is my signature and I did report this instance to the Command and to our Commander. Let me tell you that the occasion was a Physical Training session at 0630 hours that morning and Captain Johar was missing from formation, while others were present."

Prosecution additionally asked, "What evidence do you have, Sir, to prove that Captain Johar, the Defendant, altered his own Quarter's slip?"

The Major, a bit uneasy, responded, "I contacted the doctors caring for the Captain at the Kimbrough Ambulatory Care Center ("KACC") on Fort Meade. The Command has a Right to check on the well-being of its troops, as you know. One doctor stated that he had only placed the Captain on 24 hours of rest and since Captain Johar had gone to the KACC on the 4th of October then, he should have been present for the physical training in the morning of the 6th."

The Prosecutor was very thankful to Major Colors and informed him that the Board was aware that the Major had a flight to catch at 1300 hours, for which departing at 1200 hours was a must. The Major appreciated Prosecution's assurance and sat back for the cross-examination by Defense.

Phil, the Lead Defense Attorney, slowly rose to his feet and approached the Major on the Stand. The two just starred at one another for a few moments, before Phil shot into action.

Phil began, *"Major Michael J. Colors; you said that you reported Captain Arvind Johar AWOL on the 6th of October 2002, but were you aware that he was on a 72-hour Quarter's order from the KACC?"*

The Major, now, very uneasy, replied, *"Yes; obviously, I was aware that the Captain was on Quarters."*

Phil went on, *"You said that you consulted with doctors that cared for Captain Johar, but you only provided information from just one of those doctors Major. How many hours did the other doctor or doctors place Captain Arvind Johar on Quarters?"*

The Major's uneasiness was increasing exponentially and it was clearly visible. He retorted, *"I don't recall. All I know is that the Captain was required to be at physical training and he was not, which in Army life spells AWOL."*

In furtherance to his line of questioning Phil asked, *"Major Colors; it's simple, really. If one doctor said that he had placed Captain Johar on Quarters for 24 hours and that Captain was on Quarters for 72 hours then, the other doctor placed Arvind on Quarters for 48 hours. Now, if I do the math, 24 + 48 = 72; 72 hours from the 4th of October means Captain Johar was not due back to work until the 7th of October and so, on what grounds did you report our client AWOL on the 6th of October 2002?"*

There was pin-drop silence in the room for a change. Arvind was curiously observing the proceedings now. Major Colors was quiet, yet fidgeting around in his seat; Phil had dropped a bombshell, apparently. The Prosecution was all in shock and awe at its key witness' replies on cross. The Bench was serious and staring at both the Major on the

Stand and at Phil. The Legal Advisor had no clue on how to save Private Ryan this time.

Phil broke the silence. He turned to the Bench and requested, *"Please have the witness respond to Defense's question."*

The Board President, suddenly uneasy, looked at Major Colors and said, **"The witness will reply to the Defense."**

Major Colors turned to Prosecution and said, *"Jon, I thought you said I was not on trial; you assured me that I would catch my flight."*

It seemed very off-beat and very much unlike the Major to act so incoherently. For the first time, Arvind witnessed someone give Major Colors a smack of his own medicine and it felt great.

Phil took control of the situation and reiterated his question differently, "Major Colors; in-fact, your story doesn't add up at all. You claim that the Command cared for Captain Johar, but you prove by your own words that the Command has no compassion for Arvind. What, precisely, was Captain Arvind Johar seen for at the KACC on the 4th of October 2002?"

The Major replied, *"I don't recall."*

Phil reminded the Major that the Defendant had gone to the KACC with the Command's permission on the morning of the 4th of October 2002 for stomach cramps and the doctor had advised him that Arvind was suffering from a stomach virus. That doctor placed the Captain on Quarters for 24 hours and prescribed medication. That medication would make Arvind sleepy; to such extent, that the Captain was advised not to drive. Captain Johar was ordered by the doctor to return to the KACC for a check-up later at noon that day and since that doctor was unavailable; another doctor saw him and placed him on 48 hours of Quarters, which Quarters slip Arvind provided to the Command. The Head Nurse made a human error and added 24 to 48 altering the Captain's Quarters slip from 24 hours to 72 hours, without Arvind's knowledge. Captain Arvind Johar, the Defendant in this case, provided that altered form to the Command. *"So, Major; did the Captain alter his own Quarters' slip, yes or no?"* questioned Phil.

Major Colors appeared dumbfounded and lost for words; he was stuck in mud of his own making and strangely, did not know the way out. It was odd, because the Major was well-known for his knack for inventing opportunities for himself that contained elements of 'Plausible Deniability'; however, here in before this Bench, Phil had unveiled the façade behind the charges in this case; the charges were fake and false. Arvind thought, *"How will this chameleon wriggle out of this brig?"*

Phil reminded the Major that the Major was under oath to tell the truth and nothing but the truth. *"We are waiting for your response Major?"* heeded Phil.

A few seconds later; noticing no reply from the Major to Defense's cross-examination questions, Phil moved the Bench to treat this Government witness as 'hostile.'

The Board President urged Major Colors to reply to the Defense or else face the consequences, flight or no flight to catch.

Phil appealed to the Bench for an Article 32 Hearing against Major Michael J. Colors.

Prosecution objected stating that this Government witness was not charged with any misconduct.

Dave jumped to his feet and reminded the Bench that the Major was a hostile witness and refused to respond to the Defense on cross. He added that this attitude constitutes a 'breach of oath' and it would only be fair to process the Major properly through an Article 32 Hearing, as prescribed in the UCMJ.

The Defense Team was harsh now and putting on the pressure to full-throttle. Arvind contemplated, *"Will they move to an Article 32 against the Major; yes or no?"*

Dave had now taken the floor and Phil had returned to his seat next to Arvind. Dave had two documents in his hand; one he placed in front of Major Colors. Then, he asked, *"Major, Sir; the document before you is scripted by you, correct?"*

The Major replied, *"Yes."*

"In this memorandum, you state that the SCIF Manager of the Army Reserve Center on Fort Meade reported Captain Arvind Johar AWOL; is this correct, Sir?" asked Dave.

The Major responded, *"Yes."*

Dave turned to the Bench and requested that the SCIF Manager at Fort Meade be called for a telephonic cross-examination to extract the facts in this case.

The time was now almost 1135 hours and rapidly approaching noon.

The call was made and Retired Chief Warrant Officer Zimmermann (name changed) came on the line. He greeted and exchanged pleasantries in the customary manner.

Dave dug into him and asked, *"Chief; sorry for the bother. However, Major Colors has claimed that you reported to him that Captain Arvind Johar was AWOL; is this true?"*

Chief Zimmermann replied in the *affirmative*. He told the Board that the Captain was supposed to report to the SCIF, but did not arrive there.

Dave then asked, *"Was the Captain supposed to report to you Chief?"*

The Chief responded in the negative. He informed the Board that Arvind was ordered to report to the Supervisory Staff Administrator ("SSA") of the co-located sister concern.

Dave dug further into the SCIF Manager asking, *"Did the Captain report to the SSA or not Chief?"*

Retired Chief Zimmermann replied with *"I am not aware."*

Dave finally asked, *"Chief; if the Captain was not supposed to report to you then, why did you report the Captain AWOL; you were not asked to do so, so why did you report it?"*

Sensing that the Chief was cornered, he responded, *"I reported to Major Colors that Captain Johar did not report to the SCIF and Major Colors told me to report the Captain AWOL, so I did."*

Dave turned to the Bench and moved for the response of the Chief to be noted.

The Board President replied, *"So it is noted."*

The Board thanked the Chief Zimmermann and disconnected the phone.

Phil rose steadily and again moved the Bench to process the Major under the provisions of Article 32 of the UCMJ. However, Arvind sensed the Bench was reluctant to do so.

At noon, sharp, the Prosecution took the Board's permission and waved Major Colors off to the airport.

Defense moved the Bench to allow for recall of this Government witness, should there be a legal provision for the Defense to opt for an *'Article 32 Hearing'* against that witness.

The Bench noted the Defense's motion, but told the Defense counsels that it was of the opinion that Government witnesses are shielded from prosecution under the law.

The Bench asked the Legal Advisor for his guidance on the subject.

The Colonel hesitated for a few seconds and then, suggested that if the Board finds in favor of the Defendant in this case, Defense has the option to proceed separately against the Major.

A slight digression; For all those who have watched the Hollywood thriller *"A Few Good Men,"* was Colonel Jessup not processed under provisions of Article 32 of the UCMJ for ordering the Code Red against his own subordinate that killed that subordinate; then; where is the difference between that case and this one? Major Colors falsely reported Captain Johar AWOL and made others supply such false statements against the Captain. Falsifying official documents is a crime and the Major acted in disregard for the Army Officer's Code of Conduct. Shouldn't he be punished?

Back on track; with the departure of Major Colors, the Board President recessed proceedings for lunch. She made it crystal-clear that the Hearing would resume in an hour.

Jon Huddle approached Dave and informed him that the Command had ordered eight packed lunches for the Defense, if they should choose to stay back in the Headquarters.

Dave looked at Phil and declined the offer politely.

The Defense Team had lunch at the Embassy Suites, where they were staying. After lunch, the Team checked out of their individual rooms and mustered by the cars in the parking lot. The Team then drove back to the Command Post for the afternoon session.

In the Boardroom, yet again; it was the same boring routine. Defense and prosecution opposite each other and the Bench on the Stage, with the Legal Advisor seated directly opposite the Bench. If we drew a sketch of this, it would be a four-sided diamond shape. Courts are usually two parallel rows directly across from one another.

Prosecution was quick in calling his second witness; he called on LTC Caesar Augustus (name changed) to take the Stand.

Seated on the Stand; LTC Augustus greeted the Board and all exchanged pleasantries, except with the Defendant. Why was he left out; didn't he deserve to be greeted; wasn't he present in that Boardroom, or; was this exchange of pleasantries only for the superior tribe?

Prosecution swiftly went to work. Jon Huddle asked, *"LTC Augustus, Sir; in the Defendant's Officer Evaluation Report ("OER") you stated that the Defendant was the worst officer you have worked with in your entire military career; is this true?"*

The LTC replied in the affirmative. He added, *"There is no leniency in my heart for an unfit officer and the Captain failed the Army Physical Fitness Test ("APFT"), which is unforgiveable."*

"Prosecution has nothing further," indicated Captain Huddle.

Dave rose to the task for Defense this time. He slowly approached the Stand, where LTC Augustus sat keenly eyeing the young and blossoming attorney approach him.

At the edge of the Stand, with his hand on it, Dave questioned, *"Sir; Captain Arvind Johar was attached to your Command in April 2001. In May 2001, you recommend the Captain for training in December. In August 2001, post the APFT, which you graded for Captain Johar, yourself, you recommended him for the Captains' Career Course (an advanced training); because you felt that this Captain had the* wit and grit to succeed in the Officers' Corps. On September 8*th* of 2001, both the Group Commander and the RSC Commander strongly endorsed Captain Arvind Johar that Advanced Training School. Is this history accurate Colonel?"

LTC Augustus, like Major Colors prior to him, became rather uneasy in that executive chair on the Stand and visibly so. A few seconds later, he replied, *"Can you please repeat your question Captain?"*

Dave then asked the LTC whether he required a pen and paper to jot down the sequence to which LTC Augustus replied in the negative. At this; Dave repeated his question more clearly and concisely that there was 'zero' ambiguity, if there was any previously. This time LTC Augustus affirmed the chronology presented by Dave. He said, *"Yes, this is the sequence as I recall those events."*

"Well then Sir; since Captain Arvind Johar passed the Record APFT in August 2001 then, who authorized Major Colors to subject Captain Johar to another in less than six months from the August 2001 APFT; what is the Rule for the conduct of the APFT in this Army, Sir?" asked Dave.

LTC Caesar Augustus retorted, almost alike to Major Colors, *"APFT failures for us commanders are a daily task; this work is busy and a waste of valuable time for the Command, especially a Command that is earmarked to deploy in support of contingency operations. When you become a Commander, you will appreciate that which I have just imparted upon you."*

Somehow this part of the Board proceedings sounded like an interpretation of *"A Few Good Men,"* where Jessup said "You want me on that wall; you need me on that wall...."

Dave dug into this Commander now, asking him, *"Colonel; why would Captain Johar have to retake the APFT in October or November, after he passed the Record APFT in August; kindly enlighten this Board?"*

Defense was turning up the heat on these Prosecution witnesses and the Prosecutor was not amused at all.

Getting to his feet, the Prosecutor objected on the grounds of badgering the witness. Dave explained that cross-examining the Government witnesses is in compliance with both Jurisprudence and with Due Process; he made it adequately plain that questioning the LTC on the performance of the Defendant, since 'Poor Performance' was one of the four charges, was legal and Defense's constitutional right.

The Prosecutor objected again claiming that Defense was trying to mislead the Board and pull the wool over its eyes.

Dave reminded the Prosecutor that thus far, in this Hearing, evidence proved that the Government's case a rather unconvincing. Dave was not trying to rile Jon, but the truth was obvious to all in that Boardroom by now. Dave finally said, *"I hope we have not wasted the Government's time and money these last two days Captain Huddle."*

Dave returned to LTC Augustus and asked him, *"Sir; Army Field Manual clearly stipulates that the APFT for the Record will be given twice a year or once every six months. The manual also stipulates a recuperation period of four months post the Record APFT. You administered the Record APFT to Captain Johar in August 2001; you graded the Record APFT for him too. October or November 2001 is merely less than 60 days away from that Record APFT. How can a seasoned Commander like you make such an unlikely mistake Colonel, as to challenge the Rules of the Army?"*

It took LTC Caesar Augustus a few minutes to recompose himself. *He then confirmed to the Board that he had rated the Defendant in this case based on reports provided by Major Colors.* He assured the Bench that had he known about the Captain's success in the sister concern, he would have revised his ratings and requested a change to his Rating Profile.

The short of the long was that LTC Caesar Augustus admitted his mistake and was ready to fix the issues his mistake might have created for Arvind. The other major breakthrough was that LTC Augustus admitted that Major Colors was the evil behind those bizarre ratings of Arvind's performance. Earlier, Major Colors had made it amply clear that he had reported Arvind AWOL, but that Captain Johar was not actually absent; Arvind was sick in Quarters' by doctors' orders. The SCIF Manager admitted that Major Colors directed him to report Arvind AWOL, when Arvind was present for duty.

From all this legal mumbo-jumbo above, can we identify who was responsible for inventing those four charges against Arvind; who should be the 'prime accused' in this case, if not Arvind?

Remember; Captain Arvind Johar submitted an IG complaint against members of his chain of command ("COC") in February 2002, to the Inspector General ("IG") of the United States Army. This investigation was still pending in this case. Constitutional Law stipulates that the IG will protect complainants against reprisals and adverse actions, pending the outcome of investigations or inquiries by the Service IG. You must decide whether, under such Law, it is fair to subject Captain Arvind Johar to a Board of Inquiry ("BOI") on charges that arose only after he had submitted his Complaint. In Brief; was the BOI conducted in September 2003 adverse to the military career of U.S. Army Captain Arvind Johar?

If you feel that the Board was not adverse then, based on the Board proceedings above, think and share reason why you feel that the Board was not adverse to the career of U.S. Army Captain Arvind Johar. AND; if you feel that based on the Hearing, the Board adversely affected the career and livelihood of Captain Johar, in this account, then, identify the 'Intent' of the Command for convening this Board.

The Government witnesses that followed LTC Caesar Augustus were purely character destroyers. They had been selected to bring to the Board situations that would convince the Bench that Captain Arvind Johar was of poor moral fiber and thus, the Board should urge the United States Army to eliminate the Captain from service. The arguments had to be convincing beyond a doubt to attract any attention and so, the Command enlisted the services of another Lieutenant Colonel and two Majors; however, one Major would not be questioned.

"Before you go Colonel Augustus; you stated that if you had known about the Defendant's performance in the sister concern was outstanding then, you would have requested a change in your 'Senior Rater Profile' from the Army Human Resources Command ("AHRC") and, that you would have changed Captain Johar's rating on his Officer Evaluation Report ("OER"). Isn't this what you stated?" asked Phil, rising from his seat quietly.

The LTC thought and then replied, *"Yes; if the Command had informed me of the 'outstanding performance,' I would have done the needful."*

"Okay; let's take it that the Command is notifying you now and here is the evidence. Will you contact the AHRC and make the required changes?" Phil continued.

LTC Caesar Augustus was now in a bind. How will he wiggle out of it?

"I need to request my Profile from the AHRC first and then, I can place the Captain where he deserves to be" said Caesar. (The delaying tactic)

Phil was not at all impressed. He turned to LTC Augustus and asked, *"How do you rate 'outstanding performance' in the Army, Colonel? As I recall, 'outstanding performance' is usually an 'Above Center of Mass' OER or Fitness Report."*

There was silence in the Boardroom again. The attorneys of both sides were ready to spar, like Ali and Frazer decades ago. Each was waiting for the other to make that initial jab. However; neither side took advantage of the first-mover opportunity in this instance.

As Phil opened his mouth to reiterate his question to the Lt. Colonel, the Prosecution came alive with an objection.

Captain Jon Huddle retorted, *"Objection; the Defense is badgering the witness."*

Dave went to the party on this objection. He said to Jon Huddle, *"OMG Jon; Defense has not said anything and you have objected citing badgering the witness. Is this what they teach you in Law School these days?"*

The Legal Advisor, sensing another verbal brawl developing, was up at the Stand in a jiffy. He quickly took control of the situation and said to all three attorneys, *"Captain Huddle, you will quit jumping the gun. This is not your contest; there is a soldier's career on the line. As for Defense; I ask the Bench to have the last objection by Prosecution stricken from the Record, because it was unintentional. Finally; let's take a short break to refocus and return in 10."*

With that the Board President announced the recess for ten minutes and advised that Huddle's untimely objection be stricken.

The coffee break, this time, was eventful, because all Defense and Prosecution were soaking in the rays on the same platform and not a single soul spoke one work.

Ten minutes later; the Board resumed and LTC Augustus were no longer on the Stand. The fresh face of LTC Tim Dunne had taken the Stand. LTC Dunne was promoted and given Command in May 2002.

After the intro, the Prosecution asked the LTC, "Sir; based upon you own dealings with Captain Arvind Johar, the Defendant in this case, what are your assessments of this Officer?"

Dave, the proactive and aggressive Defense attorney till now, in this case, rose to his feet and objected on the grounds that personal assessments of LTC Dunne are nothing more than hearsay and inadmissible.

The Prosecution countered the Defense and argued that his intention was simply to 'break ice' with this senior field grade officer.

Dave, with the speed of light, strongly objected stating that in jurisprudence 'Hearsay' and 'Unverified Derogatory Information' have no place. This, he argued, is a strategy to try and malign the Defendant in this case and that, Dave said, is unacceptable in legal parlance.

Phil joined the party at the Stand and argued that this Board is nothing short of a 'Kangaroo Board.' He stated for the Record that Prosecution had failed miserably to prove any of the four charges thus far, in this case. Phil went on to give a thorough analysis of the Proceedings, till that time. He said that "These are the presentations of the Government witness and; given that the Prosecutor doesn't come up with other issues with the verbatim tapes in this case, you, the Bench, will realize that this Board could have been curtailed as far back as yesterday:

1. Major Colors: He submitted before this Board that the Defendant was AWOL on the 6th of October 2002.

When questioned Prosecution, Major Colors suggested that Captain Johar was absent because he failed to report for a physical training session on the morning of the 6th of October 2002.

When asked under cross-examination, Major Colors fumbled claiming CW4 (Retd) Zimmermann reported Arvind absent from the SCIF on the morning of the 6th of October 2002.

This Board then probed Chief Zimmermann asking him about Captain Johar's absenteeism and; the Chief clearly provided that Major Colors had given him direction to report the Captain AWOL.

This is the paradigm of events in this case.

Captain Johar was reporting to CW4 (Retd) Dave Janko (name changed), the Supervisory Staff Administrator of the sister concern and, not reporting to the SCIF Manager. Therefore, if Captain Johar was absent from the SCIF on the morning of the 6th of October 2002 then, the Major should have contacted Dave Janko and, not the SCIF Manager. However; more importantly, since Captain Johar had been ordered to report to the sister concern since August 2002, in this case, then whether or not the Captain was AWOL is for the sister concern to verify and, not Major Colors. Major Colors appears to have been driving this conspiracy against our client.

If this was about the missed physical training session then, Major Colors or the Admin should have contacted and communicated with Captain Johar, prior to reporting him AWOL. The Command failed to communicate.

Major Colors knew that Captain Johar was sick in quarters and the Captain's abode was on the base at Fort Meade; he should have shown compassion for Arvind by visiting him or by sending the Admin to check on the Captain's health. However, the Command did not do this either.

Instead; Major Colors took that opportunity, when the Captain was sick with a stomach virus in quarters to visit the Captain's doctors and insist on statements, which he intended to use against the Captain. This is vicious and malicious, in legal parlance.

The 3Cs of good leadership are these:

1. *Communication: Every leader must communicate openly with his subordinates.*
2. *Compassion: Every leader must care for their subordinates.*
3. *Consideration: All good leaders will consider the situation prior to taking action against his or her subordinates. Subordinates are a reflection of their leaders.*

Let me say that this Command lacks in all three facets of 'Leadership.'

The wise would know when to quit and that is at par for this case too."

Phil had said a lot and he had also made it crystal-clear that this Board was injudicious. Now; it was time for Dave to add spice to the already heated parade of jabs from Defense in this case. Even the fool would have realized that this Board was a risky business.

Dave began adding spice, as he moved gingerly towards the Stand. He said, *"Phil has carefully detailed the reason why it is wise not to have convened this verbatim Board. I only want to add that our client, Captain Arvind Johar, was not AWOL. Here is the evidence."*

Dave handed the Quarters Slip to the Board, the Prosecution and the Legal Advisor. He then went on to say, *"Yes; this is the amended Quarters Slip in question and here is the evidence to prove that our client Captain Arvind Johar did not alter his own Quarters Slip, in this case."*

Dave handed the Head Nurse's sworn statement to the Board, the Prosecutor and the Legal Advisor.

"Let me add to this" said Dave. He added, *"The doctor that Major Colors sponged a statement from said that he placed Captain Johar on 24 hours of Quarters. Here is the evidence that proves that another doctor placed our client on a separated 48 hours of Quarters, on the same day, which the Head Nurse misinterpreted as 24 + 48 = 72 hours. This is not the Captain Johar's mistake; rather, this is the mistake of the KACC. Therefore, it is unfair and unwise for this Board to find the Defendant guilty of these charges in this case."*

Suddenly; the room went abuzz with sidebars. Dave recaptured the attention of the Bench. *"Now; Ladies and Gentlemen of this Board, I will prove another misadventure of the Command in this case"* he said.

He looked at LTC Tim Dunne and said, *"Yes Sir; this one is for you."*

Dave went on, without waiting for the Bench's permission, *"LTC Dunne; according to this OER dated thru 20011028, it reads that Captain Johar was on a 'PROFILE,' which means he was medically unfit to take the Army Physical Fitness Test ("APFT") for the Record. Is this true?"*

"Roger; so I have been advised" replied the Lt. Colonel.

"Who advised you that Captain Johar had failed the APFT during that rating period, Sir?" asked Dave.

"As I recall, it was Major Colors, the CXO" responded LTC Dunne.

Dave turned to the Bench, *"Point to be noted. Major Colors told LTC Dunne that Captain Johar failed the APFT for the rating period ending 20011028."*

The Board President acknowledged.

"When did you take command of the outfit LTC Dunne?" asked Dave.

"I took command on the 29th of October 2001" replied the Lt. Colonel.

"Therefore; it is fair to conclude that the failure took place prior to your time Colonel, correct?" inquired Dave.

"Yes; I guess" responded LTC Dunne.

Dave turned to the Board and said, "I cannot believe this Command. Here is the OER dated thru 20011028, which reads that the Defendant in this case was on a 'PROFILE.' It does not state that Captain Arvind Johar failed any APFT. This is key evidence that proves Major Colors was spreading false accusations against our client in this case, as far back as 2001. This is both with a malicious and evil intent."

Finally; the Prosecution came to the party again.

"Objection; the Government witnesses are neither malicious nor evil. These witnesses are decorated field grade officers of the United States Army and this Army has placed special trust in the decision-making abilities of these leaders. It must be noted by this Board that Defense is trying to malign the good character of Government witnesses in this case" said Jon Huddle.

"Welcome Jon" groaned Dave.

Dave continued, "Defense has no reason to smear the good character of Government witnesses, but as we are evidencing that Government witnesses are damaging the good character of their own subordinate. This is evil and this is malicious, because commanders are charged with setting the example and developing the teams they have been charged to lead, coach and mentor, which the Government witnesses have failed to do so far in this case."

The Prosecutor became thunderstruck again; he seemed lost for words.

"Jon; how do you fit a square plug in a round hole?" jabbed Dave.

Dave's question had a double meaning to it, but those within the confines of this Boardroom were fatigued enough that they failed to realize the sarcasm for the asking.

Just as the tables were ready to turn against the Command, Prosecution spoke. Captain Huddle picked up a three-ring binder from his table and casually walked over to LTC Dunne on the Stand. He asked, *"Sir; this is the binder shared with Prosecution by the Command IG and I am sure you are aware of its contents. Tell this Board what you know about the IG complaint submitted by the Defendant to the Army IG."*

Instantly; Phil raised his hand. He crossly warned the Board and Prosecution, *"Objection – Subjudice material is being introduced and Defense cannot allow it."*

Prosecution retorted, *"I am confident that we are all aware that Captain Johar submitted an IG complaint against his chain of command, so there is no reason for objection by Defense."*

Phil made it undoubtedly clear, *"The Command IG requested the release of this information to prosecute our client and the Army IG denied that request. Here is the evidence."*

Dave distributed the evidence.

Phil then continued, *"The Commander of this RSC requested the release of Army IG investigative matter to prosecute our client and the Army IG denied that information for such adverse use."*

Dave distributed another piece of evidence.

Phil went on, *"The Army IG directed the Command IG and the RSC to return all investigative material to the Army IG."*

Dave distributed another piece of evidence to the Board.

Phil concluded, *"It is obvious that neither the RSC nor the Command IG did as they were directed and today, the Prosecution is trying to misuse the contents of a file, restricted for such use by the Army IG, against our client and this is not acceptable to Defense.*

The Law is relatively clear on this issue. The Law stipulates that during the course of investigations and inquiries into a Complaint, the contents of those investigative files are prohibited for use against the Complainant, unless the Complainant commits a crime. What crime has Prosecution proved, beyond a shadow of doubt, by the preponderance of the evidence? Our client has committed no crime at all. In fact; Prosecution has failed to prove any of the four charges it brought against Captain Arvind Johar in this case. Prosecution must focus on proving the four charges for which this Board was convened and, not attempt to introduce new matter that is prohibited by Law and that is not under consideration by this Board.

Where the glove does not fit, this Board must acquit – famous winning argument by F. Lee Bailey in the O.J. Simpson trial, which Defense is confident that Prosecution is aware about."

Irritated now; Prosecution strongly objected saying, *"This is not the O.J. Simpson trial and the Defense knows it. If Prosecution is not afforded the latitude to examine Government witnesses about the Defendant's IG complaint then, the Government has no case."*

Hellishly, there was pin-drop silence in the room again. The Prosecutor had stepped into muck yet again. There was no movement; the Legal Advisor did not rise this time either. The Bench was all in shock and awe, and was simply staring at Jon Huddle now. The silence lasted close to three minutes before it was broken.

Dave broke the silence saying, *"I vote for an Article 32 Hearing against Prosecution, the Command IG (his accomplice) and Major General ("MG") Karol Kenny (name changed) who is the accomplice of the Command IG. However, before proceeding, I would like to know which Command IG officer shared the Army IG investigative file with Jon Huddle."*

Defense was increasing the heat against Prosecution. LTC Tim Dunne was still on the Stand. The time was verging on thirty minutes after three in the afternoon; the Board was already 30 minutes past its target time for conclusion.

The Board President came to the rescue of Prosecution. The Colonel said, **"Are there any further question of LTC Dunne at this time?"**

Both Defense and Prosecution replied in the negative.

LTC Dunne was relieved from the Stand and he exited the room with alacrity.

The Board President ordered another ten-minute recess to use the restroom and to grab a drink, if preferred.

Defense, minus Dave, mustered around the coffee table in the rear of the mess hall. Phil gave the Defense witnesses a solid pep talk and instilled a confidence in the Team that was second to none, thought Arvind, at the time.

On return to the Boardroom, with all sides covered, the Board President directed Defense to call its first witness.

Phil and Dave both rose and moved to the center of the floor. Phil began, *"The Defense witnesses will take the Stand and give this Board a complete visual of the person; the actual character of the Defendant in this case."*

Dave added, *"Remember, it has yet to be proven, by the preponderance of the evidence, that Captain Arvind Johar* was AWOL; that Arvind altered his own Quarters Slip; that performance was poor and; that Captain Johar presented a 'Groggy Appearance' in this case."

Phil completed this Team effort by saying, *"Again; unless the glove fits our client on any of the four charges only before this Board, this Board must acquit Captain Arvind Johar of any wrongdoing in this case."*

Dave strolled back to the Defense table looking over his shoulder at Phil.

Phil called upon Army Colonel ("COL") Julia Krutz (name changed). COL Krutz was the Commander of the sister concern, under whom Captain Johar had been directed to work since August 2002.

COL Julia Krutz took the Stand and took the Oath that Prosecution served.

Phil began his examination by saying, *"Colonel Krutz; you obviously know the Defendant in this case. Since when has he been serving you in your Command?"*

The Colonel replied, *"Captain Arvind Johar was sent to us in August 2002, but he was not attached to my unit until the end of October 2002."*

Phil motioned the Bench, *"Point to be noted."*

The Board President replied, **"So noted."**

Prosecution objected on the grounds that the point made was vague and not exact.

Phil then, made it indisputably clear to Prosecution that his point was that the Command had detailed the Defendant to the sister concern in August 2002 and that the unofficial detail orders were not issued till end of October 2002, which is 60 days without legal documentation in the case of an active duty Army Officer and this is highly irregular.

Prosecution objected again on the grounds that the internal mechanisms of the Command are not on trial here.

Phil reminded the young Captain Huddle those internal mechanisms, which are known as processes are driven by procedures in the Armed Forces. He added that procedures are driven by directives and instruction from the Department of Defense ("DoD") and those DoD Directives and Instructions are driven by the Law.

Defense was showing Prosecution its rightful place in these proceedings now.

Phil continued with his examination. He asked COL Krutz, *"Kindly enlighten this Board; after Captain Johar was detailed to you, what was his performance like?"*

COL Krutz replied, *"Initially, between August and October 2002, the unit from which Arvind was detailed did not allow us to use him. They claimed he was pending charges under the Uniform Code of Military Justice ("UCMJ"). After October 2002, the performance of the Captain was such that if his security clearance was not suspended, I would have deployed him in support of contingency operations with the U.S. European Command ("EUCOM"). Arvind is an extremely bright officer, whom I can trust to get the job done. Even with tight schedules, he manages to muster support and achieves success. Arvind has assisted many of our troops in resolving their personnel admin issues with the U.S. Army Human Resources Command ("AHRC") and medical boards with the Walter Reed Army Medical Center ("WRAMC"). This is why I selected Captain Johar to spearhead the Casualty Notification and Assistance Program ("CNAP") with both the Command and with the Military District of Washington ("MDW") to prepare policy and procedures. In this assignment, he has shined too; he received a two-star letter of appreciation from the RSC Commander and from the Post Commander at Fort*

Meade. On a personal note; I will be honored to serve with Captain Arvind Johar in war or peacetime, because he is an asset to all alike."

Phil thanked COL Krutz and turned to Prosecution, "Any objections Jon?"

Prosecution answered in the negative.

Phil continued, "Colonel; kindly inform this Board what you did when you became aware that the unit from which the Defendant was detailed to you was going to prosecute him, what did you do?"

COL Krutz responded, "I asked my IG to coordinate with the Command IG to conduct an informal inquiry into the case."

Phil then asked, "Please tell us what were the findings of that informal inquiry."

Prosecution interjected and objected stating that this line of questioning was Subjudice, as there was an impending Army IG investigation.

Dave jumped into the ring to remind Prosecution that an informal inquiry was of no substance to the Army IG, yet it could assist the Army IG in reaching a conclusion in the case, with alacrity.

Prosecution then reminded Defense that it was attempting to do so with Government witnesses, but that the Defense objected and did not allow Prosecution the latitude.

Phil said, "Prosecution was trying to introduce fresh matter, which was disallowed by the Army IG, not once, but twice, I might add. Here Defense is only probing the Colonel to reach an educated conclusion about why the Defendant's performance changed so drastically between the units."

The Board President intervened and informed all, "This Board will allow Defense the latitude to question its own witnesses. Prosecution will wait for cross."

Phil asked COL Krutz to answer his question, please.

COL Krutz responded, "After Captain Johar was detailed to me, in late August 2002, I began receiving calls from Major Colors, LTC Dunne and one other field grade. All were badmouthing the Captain and placing obstacles in my approach to properly employing the Captain. The Captain denied every allegation his unit made against him and called it discrimination. Therefore; I decided to inquire into this case, in order to expose the cause for such unparalleled behavior in the Army. I tasked my IG to look into the case and to follow every rule, regulation, instruction, directive and law; I did not want my IG to suffer any failure for Arvind's sake and due to some Command compliance issue.

My IG set forth on his assigned mission and came back to me asking me if we can apply to the Command IG for an 'Informal Inquiry.' We discussed the matter and concluded that my unit will formally request the Command IG for permission to probe this case. We requested and our request was approved.

Initially; my IG contacted me telephonically, since I was out-of-state. He advised me that his initial finding was that perhaps the expectations of Major Colors from Captain Johar were far more than practical and this can appear as discriminatory.

My question to my IG was whether Arvind had simply over-reacted to Major Colors expectations or whether Major Colors was just being pig-headed.

My IG replied that Arvind is yet to complete his Officer Advanced Course, so he is not branch qualified. Therefore, to expect a non-AOC Captain to perform as a branch-qualified senior staff was improper of Major Colors. He added that

Arvind passed the APFT for the Record in August 2001 and the evidence is the Department of the Army (DA) Form signed by the unit Commander on 20010818, precisely. There is no evidence of a failed APFT.

Although this was just the preliminary, I was convinced that Captain Arvind Johar was innocent. However, as a promotable Colonel, I wanted to understand to what extent the unit leadership stretched the truth against poor Arvind, in this case. I asked my IG to share his finding with the Command IG, if appropriate, since there was a pending Army IG investigation too."

In a few words; COL Julia Krutz had supported Arvind; she was sympathetic to the innocent and; she showed her emotional side to the Bench that carried its weight in gold that afternoon. Watching the Colonel in action on his Defense earned Julia much more respect from the presently accused. **"COL Julia Krutz was indeed a true leader of troops, she cared for them; she lead them by example; she motivated them; she guided them; she coached them and; she mentored them to succeed, but, as a very last resort, maybe, this Colonel thought of eliminating members of her Team"** reveres Arvind. **"If all leaders were like her, there would be almost no threat of elimination from service"** he claims.

This is 2017 and the Board took place in 2003 – troops never forget great leaders and this is clearly evident from this story.

"My last question Colonel, before I turn it over to the Prosecution" said Phil. He asked, *"In your expert view, how would you rate the performance of Captain Arvind Johar?"*

The *objection* from Prosecution came without any delay this time. Prosecution cried out *"Hearsay."*

Phil advised the Bench that he was only asking for the Colonel's expert opinion, since the Colonel was ultimately responsible for the Captain since August 2002.

The Board President, after conferring with the other members, said, **"The Colonel will answer the question. The objection is overruled."**

COL Krutz replied, *"Captain Arvind Johar is an exceptional Army officer with a heap of talent, in my judgment. He works feverishly to achieve success, even without formal training and that is rare. I assigned him several tough projects, each with a short-fuse suspense, which he coordinated, collaborated and delivered in a timely manner. When he was sent to Advanced Schooling at Fort Huachuca in Arizona, he earned the respect of his Teams and was appreciated by the III Corps Commander too. Back on Fort Meade, as the CNAP Leader he shined and earned a two-star letter of appreciation from the Commander of this RSC, as well as from the Post Commander of Fort Meade. This is talent, which we must not destroy.*

As for this Board; in my judgment, this Board is a complete sham, because it is based upon charges that are fraudulent. Captain Arvind Johar was never AWOL and in my mind this talented officer would not even attempt such a misdeed. I could not believe it, when I was advised of the charges made against Arvind; I was nauseated enough that I contacted MG Karol Kenny to suggest that this Board was improper, but instead she threatened me with dire consequences. I even tried to meet with MG Kenny earlier today, but she denied me even a visit. This is not leadership; this is definitely denying the Defendant his due process."

As Phil turned to the Bench, Prosecution was at his heels ready to cross-examine this Defense witness. Phil said, *"Dear members of this Board, the Colonel's words in my examination are points to be noted."*

The Board President; now attentive again, said, **"Indeed; we have grasped the essence of your expert witness Phil."**

Prosecution got to work in a jiffy. *"Ma'am; we value you expert opinions in this case. Can you kindly tell this Board that if the accused had done outstanding work for you then, why have you denied him an OER so far? He has been under your leadership for over one year now"* he asked.

In reply; COL Krutz said, *"First of all Captain, the charges made against Captain Johar are mere allegations; you still need to prove these charges with the evidence. Therefore, Captain Johar is not an accused yet, so please render him his due respect.*

Second; my unit has not been allowed to process any OER for Captain Arvind Johar, since he was attached to my unit. This is because the RSC has failed to properly process Arvind's details through the Continental United States Army ("CONUSA"). This is not the fault of Captain Johar; this is a Command issue of this Regional Support Command."

Prosecution had an approach, which seemed to have gone askew. Captain Huddle continued, *"Ma'am; are you saying that the RSC is responsible for your failure to submit an OER to justify the performance of Captain Johar in this case?"*

"No; Captain Huddle, the RSC is responsible for processing all transfers, details and such matters to the CONUSA. It is not my responsibility to do so. I have tried to push the RSC Full-Time Management Officer ("FTMO") to do their job multiple times, but I can only guide the horse to water and advise it to drink; however, drinking the water is their business. Blame the apathetic attitude of the FTMO and this Command, if you so desire, but don't even try to pin the blame on me" retorted COL Krutz.

The Prosecution rested.

COL Krutz then added, *"For the Record; twisting the blame on others is an elementary fault of this Command. Instead of charging Arvind, Prosecution should be taking Major Colors and the other prosecutorial witnesses to task. The focus of this Board is perverse. Thanks."*

The Colonel exited the Boardroom with complete satisfaction that she had done her job with ease and with commendable intentions. In her heart, mind and soul Arvind was innocent and she made that vividly clear to this Board. *"Hats Off to you Ma"* chants Arvind today. COL Julia Krutz left a positive impression of Captain Arvind Johar with the Board.

Next; Dave called the Supervisor Staff Administrator ("SSA") of the sister concern to the Stand.

"Mr. Janko; kindly educate this Board on how long you have known and interacted with Arvind Johar" began the young talented Army Judge Advocate.

Dave replied, "I have known the Captain since early 2001; however, exactly when, is asking a lot."

There were chuckles all around; "Humor in Uniform at last" sighed Arvind. This change was necessary to sustain sanity within the confines of that makeshift Boardroom.

Dave continued, "Since you have known Arvind since his arrival at Fort Meade, perhaps, can you please tell this Board whether or not you believe that Arvind was AWOL and that he altered his own Quarters Slip."

"No, I did not; I cannot and; I would not believe such fairytales about Arvind at all" answered Dave Janko to Dave the Defense Counsel.

"Major Colors reported Arvind AWOL on the 6th of October 2002; are you aware of it?" asked Defense.

"Yes, I am fully aware of it" replied Mr. Janko.

Defense continued, "Do you agree with it; was Arvind AWOL on the 6th of October 2002, Mr. Janko?"

"*I totally disagree with Major Colors report and I told him so, when he came knocking on my door a few days after he submitted that report. Arvind was detailed to our unit in August 2002 and I am fully aware that he was sick with a stomach virus, in Quarters, by doctors' orders; Arvind delivered a copy of the Quarters Slip to me personally on the 4th of October. In fact; I also sent Sergeant First Class ("SFC") James Gold (name changed) to Arvind's Quarters to check on him*" replied CW4 (Retd) Dave Janko.

Dave the Defense Attorney turned to the Bench and said, "*Point to be noted; the Defendant in this case was detailed to the sister concern in August 2002 and on the 6th of October 2002 this sister concern, on two independent occasions, has clarified that Captain Arvind Johar was not Absent Without Leave ("AWOL"), because the unit to which he was attached knew he was in Quarters. Therefore; whether or not Major Colors was having a physical training session that morning is irrelevant to the Defendant in this case, because he was detailed to the sister concern over 30 days prior to that unfortunate day in history. Even the Admin would not reach out to the Captain, because the Captain was away in his books.*"

The Board President clearly stated, **"*So noted.*"**

Attorney Dave then went on, "*Mr. Janko Sir; kindly share with this Board whether or not Arvind ever presented to you or to the Colonel a 'Groggy Appearance,' please.*"

Dave Janko responded in the negative. He stated 'For The Record' that "*There is absolutely no way Captain Arvind Johar would appear groggy, fatigued or unprofessional; this is one of those fairy-tales I spoke of before. Arvind is a complete professional; a talent I have and would love to serve with, now and in the future. I believe these are the precise sentiments of the unit at-large. Arvind arrives early each day; he is counted on to unarm the alarm system, before he proceeds for his physical training. Each time he disarms the alarm, he contacts me by phone to notify me. I can count on Arvind to keep me well-informed and to share his wealth of knowledge on subjects alien to me at times. This Board is a trial of the innocent and that is injustice. Major Colors hates Arvind and this is why this Board has been convened against Arvind – what a shame."*

Prosecution was in disarray; he kept dropping pens and pencils, paper and paper-clips, as though he was nervous. Left was for the Prosecutor to start biting his fingernails; the end was in sight now.

Captain Huddle rose to his feet and shuffled his feet over to the Stand. He asked Mr. Dave Janko, *"Chief; are you aware of the IG complaint submitted by Captain Johar to the Army IG in February 2002?"*

The Retired Chief Warrant Officer replied in the affirmative. He added, *"Arvind came to seek my advice on the issue and I was clear that it is his right to Complain, if he felt his Unit did not care for him; did not communicate in a positive manner with him; did not respect him and/or; failed to honor his unblemished service to this Nation. However; this is not the appropriate place or time to discuss the Complainant's complaint, I feel."*

The Defense counsels approached the Bench, yet again, objecting to the line of question employed by the Prosecution in this case, because such line of questioning has been denied, at least twice, by the Army Inspector General earlier and Prosecution was aware of it.

The Board President was, now, very irritated. She warned the Prosecutor not to cross the fine line of privacy of the Defendant through his notorious lines of questioning.

The Board President acknowledged, *"We have been through this before Captain, so please refrain yourself."*

The Legal Advisor, who had been silent, suddenly spoke saying, *"I don't know whether this will assist any, but it appears that Prosecution is not prepared without using prohibited Army IG materials. In such a case, perhaps the Board should allow minimal latitude to Prosecution to determine his line of thinking."*

The Defense counsels objected to the subtle approval, by Legal Counsel, for the misuse of Army IG investigative materials that have been denied for such use by this Board. Phil added, *"Enough latitude has already been allowed, which may botch the ongoing Army IG case. It appears that this is the malicious intent of the Prosecutor in this case."*

Suddenly; Jon Huddle asked Mr. Janko, *"Didn't Captain Johar alter or instigate the alteration of his own Quarters Slip Chief?"*

Defense Attorney Dave strongly objected to Prosecution's question. He stated that this style of questioning is 'badgering the Defense witness.' The Judge Advocate made it clear that these questions have already been answered by the witnesses and do not require to be repeated, since this Board is verbatim.

The arguments continued and Arvind, seated at the Defense table, was witnessing every jab, counter-stab and re-dig by Prosecution in an attempt to allow him to probe his Army IG complaint. However, the Defense counsels were victorious in defending Arvind and his legal rights. Had the tables turned against the Command? Perhaps, in this Hearing Arvind had proven his innocence on all those four charges made against him in this case.

Finally; the Board President intervened and said, *"Stop fighting like kids, gentlemen; we are all adults here. Defense is right; this Board is not the correct apparatus to discuss or decide on Army IG cases. Captain Arvind Johar has rights, which the Board respects. Captain Huddle; your objection is overruled."*

Prosecution sat back down, after mentioning to the Bench that it had nothing more to ask this Defense witness. Mr. Dave Janko was released and exited the door to the rear of the room, quietly; his job here was done.

Defense called its last two witnesses, who shared with the Board the same great character image of Captain Arvind Johar. They really didn't add any spice to the trail; however, their responses imparted a perfect impression of the Defendant in this case.

There was one moment, during SFC Good's cross-examination, where Prosecution managed to mislead the experience non-commissioned officer off-course. This slight diversion may have had an impact on the Defense's presentation.

Outside of this one glitch, Defense counsels did a splendid job, recalls Arvind.

Now for the Closing Arguments in this case, which arguments was one-of-a-kind in the history of jurisprudence, perhaps. Defense led the way:

"This Board has heard all the charges, the arguments and now, it is left to your discretion, based upon the preponderance of the evidence, to decide on the fate of this outstanding talent and our client, Captain Arvind Johar.

The evidence proves that Captain Johar was never AWOL; he did not alter his own Quarters Slip, so there was no misconduct on the part of this Captain; he did not present a 'Groggy Appearance' at all and; his performance after being detailed to the sister concern was outstanding, which means, if his performance declined in any way then, it was due to the issues he suffered at the hands of his unit leadership. These were the four charges brought against Captain Arvind Johar and they were all false, as the evidence proves, in this case.

We have also heard from COL Krutz and Mr. Janko in these proceedings. Mr. Janko was clear that Major Colors hated the Captain and perhaps placed unrealistic expectations before Arvind; such that Arvind was unable to meet those impractical assignments; Arvind was denied required training, which, if he had received, he may have been successful and might have been able to stand up to Major Colors non-viable expectations. The Commander, who did nothing to resolve the matter, could have intervened to smooth the relationship between Major Colors and Captain Johar; however, these leaders failed this 15-year Veteran of the United States Army, whose impeccable record in the past five years would have seen him ascend the commissioned officer ranks. Arvind deserves another chance to prove his mettle, in a different command, under a separate commander; this is Army Regulation and we trust you will make the right decision, because Captain Arvind Johar's livelihood rides on it."

Dave sat down and Phil took his place before the Bench.

Phil added, "We all know that a number of fresh, young and newly promoted Majors and Lieutenant Commanders always try to make their first impression; mark their territory and choose only those that will remain subservient to them. Most of us in this room have witnessed it. All I say is that this is not the 'Animal Kingdom.'

Major Colors hated Captain Arvind Johar. This has been confirmed by senior members of the sister concern to which Arvind Johar was detailed since August 2002. There is no record of any APFT failure in our client's records; however, Major Colors managed to convince others that Captain Johar *failed the APFT. This he did, even though there is evidence to prove that the Captain passed the APFT for the Record in August 2001. You must choose evidence over the lies in such instances.*

In the Defendant's records; in the OER dated thru 20011028, it reads under the APFT portion that Captain Arvind Johar was on a 'PROFILE'; however, evidence proves that Arvind was only placed on PROFILE on the 4th of November 2001. The THRU date of this OER and the PROFILE date do not match. In such instances, Government must correct the OER or scrub it completely from the record. It is an injustice to the Officer to have illegitimate, inaccurate and/or inconsistent reports in his or her Official Military Personnel File ("OMPF").

Likewise; the OER dated THRU 20021029, under the 'APFT Section' reads that Captain Arvind Johar was on 'PROFILE.' This is the Defendant's Official Medical Record from the KACC on Fort Meade. Kindly find the 'PROFILE' dated in October 2002 or that was active in that same month. There is no such document in this record. There is, however, an 'APFT for the Record' scorecard in the unit files that proves that Arvind passed the APFT in August 2002. You will have to sift and choose evidence over lies, again.

This case, as you will realize, is not about AWOL, Misconduct, Performance or Appearance; you will appreciate that this case is about one man's hatred for another, whether such hatred was based on race, creed, religion or national origins is your decision.

We, the Defense, appreciate you and your time; however, these proceedings were nothing short of FW&A (Fraud, Waste and Abuse)."

Prosecution was busy scribbling notes for the 'Final Hoorah' in this case; he was so deep in concentration that

Leadership of Shame

he missed 'Closing Arguments' of the Defense. Finally; he stood before the Bench. He began, *"Whatever Defense said is inconsistent with the facts in this case; their arguments should be stricken from the record."*

Dave, the Defense Attorney in this case, jumped to his feet, *"Objection; Prosecution has no right to sully the Defense in this manner. This is highly irregular. If Prosecution wants to discredit the Defense, Prosecution must disprove Defense, beyond any doubt, by using the preponderance of the evidence."*

Jon Huddle, the Prosecutor, retorted, *"LTC Caesar Augustus reported that the accused failed the APFT for the Record then, the Defendant failed. We would be setting a bad precedence, if we begin second guessing senior leaders, like LTC Augustus, LTC Dunne and the Command IG."*

Phil joined Dave and Jon in the center of the room. He addressed Jon saying, *"When subordinates make mistakes, their superiors make those subordinates realize their mistake and assist them in fixing any issues that may have arisen due to these mistakes. Likewise; when superior officers' error or make poor decisions, subordinates help these seniors identify those errors and poor decisions. The relationship between senior and subordinate is alike to marriage; if one dislikes the other then, this relationship is doomed and this is the crux of this case, Captain Huddle."*

Even in closing, both sides were at odds with each other.

At last; Jon Huddle said to the Bench, *"Captain Arvind Johar is accused and so, you must find him guilty as charged, because this is what your Commander's wants."*

Before Phil or Dave could object, the President of the Board, for the final time, said, **"We know that Defense is in objection over Prosecution's closing statement; this has been noted. The verbatim tapes, alongside with our transcript** *and notes will be forwarded to the Army Reserve Command ("USARC"), after the RSC Commander reviews the packet and signs it. Thereafter; Defense will receive its copy in 120 days; by January 2004 end. This Board is adjourned."*

CHAPTER III

analysis of the case

The very first matter I would want to understand is the major aspects of this case and then, I would select those aspects of the case that make the most sense to me initially. When I have just one hundred and eighty days to provide an 'Initial Report of Inquiry or Investigation,' this is my approach to ensuring compliance.

My first question would be, *"On what grounds was Captain Arvind Johar eliminated/discharged from service in the Army; what was/were the charge/charges?"*

Arvind was tossed out from military service based on four charges, which were these:

1. Captain Arvind Johar was reported AWOL several times in October 2002.
2. Captain Arvind Johar presented a "Groggy Appearance."
3. Captain Arvind Johar was a substandard performer.
4. Captain Arvind Johar was guilty of "Misconduct" for altering his own quarters slip in October 2002.

My second action would be to gather all the evidence from every possible source that can either confirm or deny any or all of the aforementioned charges.

The following is what the evidence proves:
1. Major Colors charged Arvind with AWOL (absent without leave) from work on the 6th of October 2002.
2. Major Colors rescinded the AWOL charge on the 9th of October 2002.
3. Major Colors, again, charged Arvind with AWOL on the 14th of October 2002.
4. Major Colors rescinded the AWOL charge on the 16th of October 2002.
5. The Army Critical Care Command on Fort Meade confirms that Arvind reported sick with a stomach virus on the 4th of October 2002 and his Doctor recommended rest and recuperation for 24 hours. This Doctor also recommended that Arvind return to the Army Critical Care at noon that same day for a follow-up. Arvind received his quarters slip and shared it with his concerned leaders and his Unit Administrator.
6. At noon, on the 4th of October 2002, Captain Johar returned to the Army Critical Care Command on Fort Meade, as recommended by his Doctor. The same medical specialist could not see Arvind, so another Doctor conducted the follow-up and recommended that the Captain remain in quarters for 48 hours. A copy of this Medical Consult Sheet was shared with the concerned leaders and Arvind's Unit Administrator, as he had done earlier.
7. Instead of providing Arvind with a fresh quarters slip, the Head Nurse simply altered Arvind's initial quarters' slip, which was an oversight on the part of

the Head Nurse; this was a lackadaisical approach that backfired.

8. Major Colors, on receiving the altered quarters slip, didn't waste any time in blaming Captain Arvind Johar for the Head Nurse's mistake. He raced from the Command headquarters to the Army Critical Care Command on Fort Meade and began gathering statements he intended to use against Arvind. This the Major did without the knowledge of Arvind.

9. A junior federal civil service staff assigned at the Army Critical Care Command on Fort Meade gave Major Colors a written statement. In this statement the GS-06 wrote that Captain Arvind Johar visited the Army Sanatorium on two separate occasions, on the 4th of October 2002, which was accurate. However; this federal civil service employee was not involved in the treatment of Captain Johar in any way.

10. The Doctor that first saw Arvind in the morning of the 4th of October 2002 wrote a statement at the behest of Major Colors. The Doctor wrote that the he had recommended Arvind rest and recuperates at home for 24 hours. This statement is accurate, but it doesn't address the second Doctor Captain Arvind Johar saw on follow-up at noon that same day.

11. The Head Nurse, as well, provided his written statement in which he admits that he made a mistake of adding the first quarters' recommendation with the second to arrive at 72 hours on quarters.' He admits his fault and clarifies that Arvind had nothing, at all, to do with the alteration of the Captain's quarters' slip. The Head Nurse apologized

saying he had no idea that his error would be bent out of proportion in such a manner.

12. The only two negative performance appraisals on Arvind's Official Military Personnel File ("OMPF") were those submitted by the Command against which Captain Johar had complained. The reports from sister concern to which Arvind was detailed only reported the Captain's helpful attitude and outstanding performance. The reports prior to Arvind assignment to the Command were superb and outstanding. Hence; it appears that the performance appraisals from the Command against which Arvind complained are in isolation.

13. "Groggy Appearance" is a fancy usage of words that simply means tired and fatigued appearance. Arvind had been fighting against accusations from his leadership for almost a year and anyone in such a predicament would become fatigued and tired; this is alike to fighting against an institution that dislikes those who choose to complain against their leaders. However; being tired or fatigued is not reason enough to eliminate or discharge subordinates.

Now; the following are my findings, based on the evidence gathered:

1. Captain Arvind Johar was not AWOL; the Captain was sick in quarters, on recommendation of doctors. The fact that the Head Nurse faltered by providing Captain Johar with an altered slip was no fault of Arvind's at all. Arvind felt he had 72 hours on quarters. The Captain resided on Fort Meade and saw the doctors at the Army Critical Care Command on Fort Meade. Military officers do fall ill; it is natural, but it is no reason to send an officer to trial

or eliminate him or her. Thus; Captain Arvind Johar was not AWOL at all.

2. Captain Arvind Johar did not alter his own quarters' slip; the Head Nurse altered the slip without the knowledge of the sick Captain and, the Head Nurse has admitted it, in writing. The GS-06 has verified that Captain Johar saw doctors twice on the 4th of October 2002. One of these two doctors has verified that he recommended Arvind to rest in quarters' for 24 hours. There is another Medical Consultation Form, signed by another doctor, confirming that she recommended Arvind rest in quarters for 48 hours. There is no question that there was no 'Misconduct' on the part of Captain Arvind Johar in this case. There is further no reason to have sent this Captain to trial or to have eliminated him from service on this accusation either.

3. Poor performance was isolated to the Command against which Captain Arvind Johar had submitted his Complaint. Prior to and after this Command of Isolation the Captain's performance was reported as superb and outstanding. Army Regulation stipulates that in order to properly rehabilitate poor performance in one Command, the affected officer must be transferred to a different command to serve under a separate commander. In Arvind's case, the Command detailed him to a sister concern and, did not transfer him. There appears to be a compliance issue on the part of the Command, as well. Therefore; I conclude that if there was poor performance then, Captain Arvind Johar was not allowed to properly rehabilitate to prove his mettle. Arvind is an officer with over a decade of active

duty service and, by and large, his performance has been solid, great and outstanding. Everyone has a hiccup or two, yet none of these hiccups are grounds for trial or reason to eliminate talent.

4. The last is "Groggy Appearance." Fatigue or tiredness of military personnel is not an anomaly at all; fatigue can be caused by many factors, personal or professional. In this case, the tiredness could have been from fighting an attacking command. However; there is no evidence in Captain Arvind Johar's military record to prove he presented such an appearance ever. Subjective and uncorroborated accusations are no grounds for trial or elimination; hearsay and unverifiable allegations are no reason for trial and elimination either.

In summary; I would write the following:

1. Was Arvind Johar absent without leave in October 2002? No.
2. Did Arvind Johar alter his own quarters' slip in October 2002? No.
3. Was the poor performance isolated to the Complainant's Command? Yes.
4. Did Arvind Johar present a "Groggy Appearance"? No; there is no such evidence.
5. Was there sufficient grounds by the preponderance of the evidence to convene a trial against Arvind Johar? No.
6. Was it proper to have eliminated/discharged Arvind Johar from the United States Army and Army Reserves? No; not at all.

The abovementioned would have been my 'Interim Report of Investigation' surrounding the BOI convened against Captain Arvind Johar in September 2003, in this case; short, sweet and precise. I would also append all the evidence I gathered and share it with the Captain, ahead of submitting my report to the Inspector General of the Army for review.

The second matter I would tackle is the EMHE and the MHEs, recommended and conducted by the Command under investigation in this case. My intent would be to confirm or deny the fact that the EMHE and MHEs were not recommended or done in reprisal against Captain Arvind Johar and that these Command activities were not premeditated either. After all; Captain Arvind Johar reported that the EMHE conducted against him in October 2002 was premeditated in reprisal. Arvind reported this to the Army IG in November 2002.

First; I would want to know the number of Mental Health Evaluations ("MHE") done and recommended by the Command under investigation. The "EMHE" is an MHE done under Emergency conditions.

I find that the Command under investigation ordered Arvind to a MHE in October 2001. The Command under investigation then, recommended Arvind for another MHE in May 2002. Finally; in October 2002, the Command under investigation ordered and sent Arvind for a second MHE, under Emergency conditions. Therefore; in a period of one year, the Command under investigation conducted two MHEs: One regular and one under emergency conditions. This Command also recommended Arvind for another MHE in May 2002, but that recommendation was denied.

My next adventure would be to capture the essence of the basis upon which these MHEs were conducted and recommended. The evidence states this:

1. The MHE for which Captain Arvind Johar was sent to in October 2001 was done on the basis of a non-military third party. This non-military third party informed Major Colors alone that Arvind was abusing prescribed medication which was in the form of steroids. My questions are these: (a) how this non-military third party knows that the Captain was abusing prescribed medication and; (b) why did this non-military third party only share her accusation with Major Colors and; (c) why did the Major send Arvind for the MHE without verifying? Definitely, there was something wrong. So; I probed the Doctor, who has over 25 years of expertise in his medical profession.

2. The Doctor with 25 years of expertise conducted the MHE and found Captain Arvind Johar in sound health and mind. He suggested to Major Colors, in writing, that the Major should refrain from interfering in his medical practice. The Doctor made it crystal-clear that his medication was administered by his staff, in his office, under medical compliances, with his consent. He further suggested that the non-military third party had approached him too and, the Doctor's assessment was that this non-military third party was aggrieved and would go to any length to retaliate. Hence; it was clear to me that the MHE conducted against Captain Arvind Johar on orders from Major Michael J. Colors was an unsound decision. I got a copy of that letter from the Doctor to Major Colors from the Doctor.

3. I found that the recommendation for a second MHE, in May 2002, was made because Major Colors

was "fumed" at Captain Johar for submitting an IG complaint, in which the Major was named as the prime accused. The Command also recommended that following the recommended MHE Captain Johar should be "detailed" to the sister concern for six months. In the military, six months equates to 179 days. My question was how did Major Colors come to know that Captain Johar had submitted an IG complaint? The evidence contained the abuse of prescribed drugs again, which I found to be false earlier.

4. Evidence shows that after Captain Johar submitted his IG complaint to the Army IG, the Army IG pawned its responsibility to investigate on the Inspector General ("IG") of the United States Army Forces Command ("FORSCOM"). The FORSCOM IG further pawned its responsibility on to the IG of the United States Army Reserve Command ("USARC") and; the USARC IG pawned that investigative responsibility on to the Command IG, who, arbitrarily closed the case and compromised the case file through the non-military third party. The non-military third party then, opened the packet addressed to Arvind and shared its contents with Major Colors alone, who became "fumed" at the Captain. My question is who was responsible for the compromise; is it the Command IG or is it the Army IG?

5. The MHE done under Emergency a condition (the "EMHE") in October 2002, according to the medical specialists at the Army sanatorium on Fort Meade, was done for the following reason: "The XO said that Captain Arvind Johar was psychotic or manic,

because he submitted a 130+ pages IG complaint/ Request for Investigation against his COC in Feb 2002." The XO was none other than Major Michael J. Colors and the COC was the chain of command under investigation, in this case. You, my readers, decide whether the reason for the EMHE was reprisal, based upon that statement provided by the medical specialists.

6. I found that Captain Arvind Johar only submitted an eight-page IG complaint against his chain of command, in which the XO was the prime accused. I did not find any evidence to confirm that Arvind submitted 130+ pages to the Army IG at any time in this case.

7. I further found that the Command IG had made a statement to medical specialists at the Army sanatorium on Fort Meade, before or after the XO. She claimed that Arvind contacted her and made a "Bizarre Statement" to her. This was the same Command IG that earlier closed Arvind's case arbitrarily and compromised his case file. What statement did Arvind purportedly make to his Command IG ahead of the EMHE in October 2002?

8. According to the Command IG, Arvind Johar called his Command IG on the morning of the EMHE and suggested that his Command wanted to kill him; that his Command was going to have him tied, abused and beaten. However; the Command IG provided no evidence of the call and so, I can only report this as 'Hearsay.' Although; if Arvind had called his Command IG and reported this aforesaid matter, I would assume he feared the actions of his leadership. In addition, I found that Arvind was

handcuffed before he was taken to Walter Reed Army Medical Center ("WRAMC") in the nation's capital. I further found that he was manhandled and refused due process. Arvind was kept in solitary confinement for five of those eight days to beat him into submission. As such; if the Captain had made such a statement then, his statement was honest and, not "Bizarre," at all.

9. After the EMHE, the Command arbitrarily, without proper approvals, "detailed" Arvind to the sister concern for 179 days, exactly as it was recommended in May 2002, when Major Colors was "fumed." You decide whether this EMHE followed by the 179-day detail to the sister concern, within the same Command, was premeditated or accidental.

The reason to conduct the MHE under Emergency conditions against Captain Arvind Johar in October 2002, based upon the Medical Report prepared by the Army Critical Care Command on Fort Meade, was definitely reprisal for submitting an IG complaint against members of the chain-of-command ("COC") in February 2002. Major Colors made this statement to medical specialists himself, without any provocation and of his own free will.

The Law, as provided under Section 546 of Public Law 102–484 (1992), in the United States of America, clearly stipulates that no uniformed service member that includes the Armed Forces will be subjected to an involuntary Mental Health Evaluation, in reprisal, for communicating with an IG or with a Member of Congress. This Public Law is available on the website of the Surgeon General of the Army and Army Reserves.

Along with the Public Law, the United States Department of Defense ("DOD") has implemented Directive 6490.1, in which, under Paragraph 4.3.2, it clearly stipulates that no person may refer a service member for a mental health evaluation as a reprisal for making or preparing a lawful communication with a Member of Congress, an IG, and a law enforcement organization.

Paragraph 4.3.4 of DOD Directive 6490.1, which applies to all the branches of the Armed Forces in the United States of America, to include the Army, stipulates that violation of any part of Paragraphs 4.3.2 and 4.3.3 is subject to the Uniform Code of Military Justice ("UCMJ"), under Article 92.

Article 92 of the UCMJ stipulates that anyone who fails to obey a general order or regulation is derelict in the performance of his duties; shall be punished by court-martial.

Major Colors was not charged under Paragraph 4.3.2 or 4.3.4 of DOD Directive 6490.1, as he should have been for having a mental health evaluation conducted against Arvind Johar for submitting an IG complaint and for communicating with an Army IG.

Instead; in 2009, which is over seven years after the incident, the Army claimed that the Commander and, not Major Colors, "pleaded ignorance of the law." Obviously, the Army was covering-up for Major Michael J. Colors in this case. This is alike to pleading ignorance of the law after having sex with a minor, whether consensual or not; the law doesn't allow it.

However; the honorable Courts in the United States of America will ask whether the mistake of involuntarily sending Arvind Johar for the mental health evaluation under emergency conditions in October 2002 was necessary or not and, could it have been delayed by 48 hours to comply with the Law.

The Army would argue that delaying the involuntary emergency mental health evaluation was not possible based on the "Bizarre Statement" proposed by the Command IG

Arvind's Defense Team would argue that the "Bizarre Statement" was never made, but that it provides debatable reason to evaluate; the matter in the statement is neither clear nor convincing and there is no evidence to corroborate it. And; such evaluation did not need to be eight days. Additionally; it must be noted that the Command IG presented such "Bizarre Statement" about a Complainant it was purportedly investigating and this presents a conflict of interest in this case. Further; the Army did not have to deny our client his due process rights and violate Paragraph 4.3.2 of DOD Directive 6490.1 and Section 546 of Public Law 102–484 (1992).

In the United States Armed Forces; when someone submits a Complaint against actions of the members of his or her chain-of-command, the Complainant is labeled a 'Whistleblower' and if the matter is mishandled, and compromised, it sparks reprisals against the Whistleblower. This is why the Congress of the United States of America enacted the 'Whistleblower Protection Act,' which is stipulated under Section 1034 of Title 10 of the United States Codes. This Act stipulates that no person shall restrict a member of the Armed Forces from communicating with members of Congress and the Inspector General. This Act also stipulates that no one shall threaten or take adverse actions against a person of the Armed Forces, who have made a protected communication with a member of Congress or the Inspector General. My question to you, my readers, is was the mental health evaluation under emergency conditions done in violation of the 'Whistleblower Protection Act'?

The above is Constitutional Law. The DOD Directive which is derived from the Constitutional Law is DOD Directive 7050.6 and this prohibits adverse actions against those that make a Complaint against members of their commands. My question is whether the EMHE and the trial; the BOI conducted against Arvind Johar in September 2003 legal, since the Army IG was, supposedly, still investigating this case?

I believe that the United States Army deliberately undermined Captain Arvind Johar's case; the Army IG never actually investigated his Complaint or the reprisals. However; the Army fudged a report and made excuses to cover-up it's dereliction of duties. In brief; the glove does not fit at all.

CHAPTER IV

conclusion

This is a true account of what actually transpired in the United States Army from September 2001. The names have been altered, changed or amended to protect the actors. Your assessment and feedback may help Captain Arvind Johar, finally, get honored for his services in uniform. We sleep comfortably at night, because our heroes in uniform keep watch over our nation and its interests. We celebrate the Armed Forces for the sacrifices they make, voluntarily, and for their bravery and for their selfless service. Does Arvind Johar not deserve to be honored; does he not deserve our respect didn't Arvind stand watch for the safety and security of the nation?

In March 2004, Arvind was discharged from active duty in the Army, based upon the Board convened against him in September 2003 and in October 2004; Arvind was retried at a second Board of Inquiry, based upon the same four charges listed herein. My question is was this not 'Double Jeopardy'; can a person be tried twice based on the same set of charges in the United States of America?

Double Jeopardy in the United States means being tried twice for the same offence and it is strictly prohibited by Law, under the Fifth Amendment of the Constitution of the United States.

In March 2005, Arvind was eliminated from service based on the Double Jeopardy board convened against him in October 2004.

Based on the evidence and the facts in this case; I do not believe Captain Arvind Johar deserved to be tried or eliminated from service. I believe the Army goofed-up and then, has been attempting to cover-up its mistakes to avoid condemnation from the public.

In 2012, the Government Accountability Office I the United States investigated the Armed Forces and found that the Inspectors General of the services arbitrarily closed cases due to overload of complaints. Hence; many officers and soldiers were willfully affected and a large number lost their livelihoods. When you study this case, you find that Arvind may have been a victim of this willful negligence and dereliction of duties of the Army IG.

I leave you, my readers, to examine this case again and reach your own conclusions. As I have said, your feedback is valuable to the cause of getting Arvind what he actually deserves.

Before I depart, I will be amiss not to impart to you that military or not, leadership is the same everywhere. Keep your internal matters at home private and don't mix personal and professional lives, because the two make for a volatile explosion that can result in harm only. I will also appeal to leaders not to meddle in the private lives of your subordinates, no matter how compelled you may be to do so, because your interference can be construed as an inappropriate affair. People gossip and walls have ears. This case depicts a "Leadership of Shame," whereas; "Rise to Fame" depicts leaderships of honor that encouraged subordinates, like Arvind to succeed and that gave him room to make mistakes and advance his leadership skills. These are true accounts to help choose the best leadership style for our budding professionals and our already established brass.

Thank You.

www.ingramcontent.com/pod-product-compliance
Lightning Source LLC
Chambersburg PA
CBHW020452220526
45464CB00002B/963